Hook, Lyin´ & Sinker

ALSO BY BRIAN R. PETERSON

The Great Duck Misunderstanding
Laugh It Up in Deer Camp

Hook, Lyin' & Sinker

A Tangle of Fishing Humor

Compiled by
Brian R. Peterson

Essex, Connecticut

An imprint of Globe Pequot, the trade division of The Rowman & Littlefield
Publishing Group, Inc.
4501 Forbes Blvd., Ste. 200
Lanham, MD 20706
www.rowman.com

Distributed by NATIONAL BOOK NETWORK

British Library Cataloguing in Publication Information available

Library of Congress Cataloging-in-Publication Data

Names: Peterson, B. R., compiler.
Title: Hook, lyin' & sinker : a tangle of fishing humor / compiled by Brian R.
  Peterson.
Other titles: Tangle of fishing humor
Description: Essex, Connecticut : Lyons Press, [2023] | Includes bibliographical
  references. | Summary: "A collection of the best and funniest jokes and cartoons
  about fishing, with special emphasis on bass fishing (and gear) and fly fishing.
  Companion outdoor book to *Laugh It Up in Deer Camp, Hook, Lyin' & Sinker*
  is an unusually rich collection of fishing humor not found elsewhere. A good
  humor book for those of good humor, smartly curated for all ages and genders.
  It's for people who may or not fish who need a laugh or want to give a laugh
  to friends and family members who fish any water, any fish species, and any
  technique"— Provided by publisher.
Identifiers: LCCN 2023018031 (print) | LCCN 2023018032 (ebook) | ISBN
  9781493074631 (trade paperback) | ISBN 9781493074648 (epub)
Subjects: LCSH: Fishing—United States—Humor.
Classification: LCC PN6231.F5 P45 2024 (print) | LCC PN6231.F5 (ebook) |
  DDC 818/.5402—dc23/eng/20230601
LC record available at https://lccn.loc.gov/2023018031
LC ebook record available at https://lccn.loc.gov/2023018032

To Bruce Cochran, grand master cartoonist and outdoor humor writer, who brought great joy to those who play outdoors. RIP 2022.

Contents

Compiler's Note

The compiler would like to apologize for the following errors that appear in this very collectible first edition. Page numbers may not be accurate either. Corrections will appear in the second edition, which is equally unlikely.

Page 23: Delete "Catching fish isn't important, just being there is."

Page 62: Fish sticks are *not* supposed to have scales.

Page 90: Ocean fish pulled from an oil spill need less cooking oil.

Page 104: Under outdoor hygiene: Add "A waste is a terrible thing to mind."

Page 118: Under Tips for Swedish Ice Fishermen: "Fishing ice rinks is not very productive but there is no competition from non-Swedish fishermen."

Page 131: Wearing hemp-based underwear will not get you high.

Page 140: Under Fly-Fishing Apparel, insert "Fly fishermen dress left."

Page 146: The medical use of marijuana for fishing-related illness is legal in most states, especially Oregon.

Page 162: Drinking like a fish is the first step in a twelve-step big-mouth program.

Page 180: Monkfish is the Friday entrée at the abbey.

Introduction

$\mathcal{F}$ishing is silly business. Everyone knows but rarely admits that it's a lot easier and much less expensive to buy fish at the local supermarket. However, the fishing business isn't silly when you look at what is spent on fishing every year. Fishing contributes little toward world peace. For that matter, in many households, fishing rarely contributes toward domestic peace either. But so what? Fishing is more fun than writing code, cleaning toilets, a prostate exam or mammogram, or homework for junior anglers. And chores. Feel free, dear reader, to add to this list.

I first fished with a cane pole, enough line, a red-and-white round bobber, and angle worms, along the shore of a lake in a city park in a small town in north central Minnesota. Cheap entertainment. My first Mepps lure was purchased with squirrel tails. I would fish most of the day if I brought a sandwich. The catch was small perch and too often and unfortunately a small bullhead. After a while, you knew just by the bite which was jerking your line. The perch, easy to catch and clean, were keepers. Bullheads, however, seemed like freaks of nature. Whiskers on a fish were like a mustache on a nun. (And usually ended up in Mom's rose garden.) These early days were simple, even as you added minnows, rods, and reels, and flashy Daredevles®. From then on, everything else is an exaggeration of those early summer days fishing.

The common thread through my time on the water was fun—home of funny. We were lucky; fishing wasn't a chore, necessarily. If the stringer was empty, the family still ate well. Fishing did feel important, though. It was a skill that could merit a Cub Scout badge. And as you grew up in the sport, fishing never lost its novelty. In the best of circumstances, fishing can't be more fun and the people who fish can't be funnier, especially in the worst of circumstances: with a hook in your—even better, *their*—ear. There are two groups of people who find fishing and fishermen funny: those who fish and those who don't. Those who do find joy, camaraderie, a world at peace; while those who don't use stereotypes to shape their perception. Those who fish know the reasons to fish; the others don't know the freedom of spending a few hours doing what appears to some to be almost nothing at all.

Fishermen easily fit public stereotypes. That perception is mostly good-humored, but even barbed, those who fish can take a hit. What's interesting is that the words "a fisherman" can be inserted and fit in the great non-fishing jokes. For example, if you describe the character in this innocuous tale as a fisherman, it seems funnier:

> *Once there was a boy named Odd. He was the butt of jokes his entire life because of his name. Eventually he grew up to be a very successful fisherman and even owned fish-processing plants. When Odd was about ready to die, he asked, "People have been teasing me all my life and I don't want them doing that after I'm dead, so please don't put my name on my gravestone." After Odd died, people saw his blank tombstone and said, "That's odd."*

This collection of fishing "jokes" can be described as a carnival. Little organization. Few chapter heads. Nobody is safe. No echo chambers. A big mess of fishy material. A "cacklebox" of one-liners, stories, and good-humored narratives. Even a very fine parody. Some of the best material comes from former newspaper reporters who lived the sporting life and reported with great wit and craft. In a spare moment, tip your hat to those professionals who have been replaced by "outdoor/ sports" writers who only file team-sport reports with minuscule personal relevance. Of course, early virtuosos of outdoor humor from the back pages of heritage magazines live on in book collections (Ed Zern from *Field & Stream*, Patrick McManus from *Outdoor Life*), and Bill Heavey's comic musings are current and collectible. This collection is also a celebration of the great cartoonists (now more past than present) that expand the great humor narratives.

Henry Beard, co-founder of the *National Lampoon* magazine, once remarked, "It's just so difficult to write humor in print." It's equally hard to draw good humor, but the contributors presented within have tried their best to make you laugh about their and your favorite sport. Tight lines, everyone!

P.S. Look at it this way: Fishermen take a lot of guff, but who would you rather have as a neighbor—a fisherman or a lawyer? (Especially a fisherman running out of freezer space.)

You don't know generosity until you meet a generous fisherman.

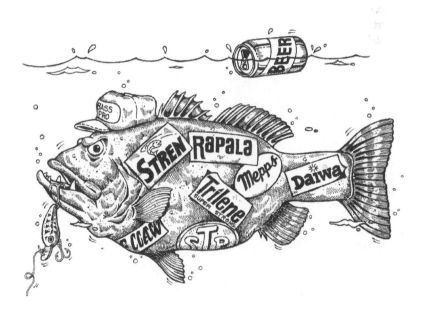

Ex-Angler Is Surviving in a Vegetative State

"Anybody home?" I asked, rapping on the door.

I was visiting my good friend and a former fishing fanatic, Milt Axelroot. His wife, Sunflower Moonglow Kowalski-Axelroot, after an epic battle that lasted years, had converted Milt to vegetarianism a couple of months before. I thought I'd stop by and see how it was going.

Coming from the backyard was a swishing sound followed by the rending and tearing of plant life, much like the noises you hear on a National Geographic special when a herd of stampeding elephants flattens a banana plantation.

Peering around the corner of the house, I saw Milt, clad in waders and fishing vest, standing in his daughter's wading pool and making false casts over the garden with his favorite nine-foot, light-action graphite fly rod.

"Hi, Milt, how's it going?" I asked cheerily.

"Shhhhh," he said angrily. "You'll spook the cukes."

He launched a greenish fly into a tangle of vines, mended the slack, then reared back on the rod.

An eleven-inch cucumber, impaled on the No. 6 hook, tore loose from a vine and wobbled and rolled across the lawn as Milt reeled in.

He scooped it up in a small trout landing net, detached the hook, admired it for a moment, then placed it gently into a wicker creel at his waist.

"A couple more like that and we'll have a dandy salad," Milt said with a grin. "I took a four-pound casaba from the same spot a couple of weeks ago," he added, gesturing toward a dirt mound of melon

"...don't let him horse you in! Wiggle your tail! That's it! Now jump!..."

vines. "It was tricky getting it in, though. It wrapped the line around a sprinkler head while I was fighting it."

"I see you've made the adjustment to being a nature nut-loaf," I observed as Milt began false-casting again, shifting his position in the wading pool.

"Yeah. It was tough. When Sunflower told me I'd have to give up fishing and hunting, the marriage almost went into the dumper. But with little Lotus Ankh just turning four, and the community-property laws being what they are, this seemed like a more acceptable compromise."

"It wasn't easy at first," Milt added after a moment, allowing the line to shoot out into the garden.

He said he had to set up his fly bench to tie tomato horn worm and apple maggot imitations.

And it was during one outing to test the apple flies that the police arrested him casting over an abandoned Grannie Smith orchard near Corvallis, Milt said.

His explanation to the officers led to a seventy-two-hour hold for psychiatric observation at the Oregon Home for the Bewildered, he continued. But once Sunflower showed up and explained what was going on, the justice system relented.

Since then, Milt told me, things have been going along pretty smoothly. "I caught a mess of tomatoes with a couple of cabbage butterfly imitations this morning," he said. "A couple of them were pretty small, but I had to keep them because they were pulp-hooked."

Milt said he was pretty busy most nights tying up his assortment of agricultural pest imitations for his upcoming vacation. The family was planning a tour of U-pick farms in northeastern Oregon and southern Washington, he explained.

"Missing real fishing isn't so bad," Milt said, a shade of wistfulness in his voice. "Hell, next week I'm going out on a charter boat out of Depoe Bay to go kelp fishing.

"And a healthy-sized kohlrabi or carrot will give you a good fight trying to get it out of the ground, especially on light tackle."

Milt began false-casting again over a likely looking stand of pole beans, which he referred to as the panfish of the vegetable kingdom.

"It takes a mess of them to make a meal," he said, detaching a wax bean from the hook and adding it to the creel.

*"You wouldn't believe the guy I just got away from!
I'll bet he weighed 300 pounds!"*

I decided to leave him to his fun, but I couldn't resist asking just one more question. "Milt, I can see you've adjusted pretty well to being a compost head when it comes to fishing," I said. "But you were such a hunting fanatic. How did you learn to live without that?"

A grin spread on his face from ear-to-ear. "Come on inside the house," he said, reeling up the line and tucking the fly rod under his arm. "I'll show you my fourteen-pound watermelon. I had the rind mounted.

"I got it right through the stem at a hundred and fifty yards. Didn't ruin any of the meat."

2

Fishing with Your Dad, Again

If you're a decent, right-thinking American, your dad most likely taught you how to fish. He escorted you to some dinky slough or ditch-water populated by bluegills, sunnies, and crappies, and you heaved the poor little minnows out of the water like a guy on a tuna trawler. As you aged, Dad may have introduced you to more elaborate fishing events such as bass fishing, drifting for walleyes, or, if Daddio was an ironist or a sadist with a strange sense of humor, fly fishing.

There always comes a moment in a fisherman's life when he believes—no, he knows!—that his fishing expertise has outstripped his father's.

"The silly old dodderer," you may mumble. "He's just not up to speed on all the latest innovations and the new fishing tech. I'll take the geezer out and introduce him to the *New World of Fishing Gear* and Attendant Silicon Valley Electronic Gizmos."

The quiet attempted overthrow of Dad as Your Personal Jedi Bassmaster is underway. You download the Nightcrawler app on your iPhone equipped with Personal Range Finder/Fish ID, and you covertly snicker about showing up the old goat.

"Gee, Dad, Lazy Ikes went out with, well, Ike. I mean, that's right out of *Leave it to Beaver*. Come on, man . . . I'll get you the hookup with these chartreuse LED, acai-flavored plugs with neon landing lights."

Dear Old Dad tells you to kiss his ass and ties on the antiquarian Lazy Ike, shaming you, and gratuitously allows how "this worked during the Cuban Missile Crisis and it'll work this morning."

At the end of the day, you and your fishing app and your acai-chartreuse LED lure are 0 for 4. Meanwhile, Pops is making the boat list to starboard because his full stringer weighs what you weighed in high school. *Father Knows Best* is back on the air, baby.

Tips from Your Guide

- The American Fishing Tackle Manufacturers Association forbids catching fish with your own hands.
- Parcel post is the least expensive way to ship fish across the country to your brother-in-law.
- Some resorts have a cast-and-blast program, which seems to suggest you can shoot fish. Check with guides as to which firearms to bring.
- Wood-oar handles can be rough and have splinters. Make sure your wife has a pair of good rowing gloves.
- Be careful in bear country. Tie the day's catch to the upwind pole on your mother-in-law's tent.
- Have your wife vary the boat speed while rowing. Erratic speed will cause your lure to act more like a live bait fish.
- A bar on a lake is a good place to fish. Not a bad place off the lake, either.
- Be thoughtful on opening day. A carpet remnant tacked to the bottom of the boat makes an ideal break area for your rowing wife.
- "Lute" in lutefisk means "Odin's soiled shorts" in Old Norwegian.
- Adding untreated stream water to your mother-in-law's whisky will prepare her for an early departure from the camp-family reunion.
- Maggots will hatch if not refrigerated. Keep them in the little woman's yogurt.
- Petition your cable company to add *This Old Ice House,* a program bursting with tips on how to remodel your home away from the house.

• 4 •

Channel Fishing

*W*hen our son was young, my wife and I had no television. We wanted our boy to become a reader, not a viewer. Our plan was largely successful, except for one babysitter who not only had a TV set but believed her viewing was vital to keep *Little House on the Prairie* in syndication.

When we finally bought a TV, the antenna on our coastal-Virginia roof could pick up only two networks clearly and two public broadcasting stations fuzzily. That was okay, since I mainly watched local weather forecasts to determine when it'd be safe for me to run offshore in my seventeen-foot Whaler.

Then I began doing some documentaries for public television on decoy-carving and angling history. After our accountant told me I was doing enough TV work to qualify for a deductible upgrade on our reception, I acquired a satellite system.

What a revelation! One channel selling junk jewelry twenty-four hours a day; another featuring "celebrities" no one over thirty has ever heard of; still others devoted to cartoons, silly games, and over-seasoned food. But then I also found channels for the likes of me, featuring classic movies, science, history, wildlife, travel, and—especially—fishing. Yet because I have some familiarity with these subjects, I soon noticed that the medium's appetite for moving images always takes precedence over accuracy, thoughtful dialogue, and even—occasionally—ethical behavior.

One wet and windy morning, I recorded snippets of conversation from all the angling shows I could find on several different channels and then blended them into a single make-believe outing. Every cliché that follows was spoken during one or more shows. Only their sequence has been rearranged. Henceforth, any viewer who loses the audio portion of a fishing show can use this as a guide to find out what the anglers are saying.

So long as they're fishing, but not catching: "Does it get any better than this?—The answer to a prayer—I wonder what the poor people are doing—I feel sorry for people who never see stuff like this—Sweet stuff.—What a place!—Amazing!—Absolutely amazing!—I can't believe it—You better believe it—I'm speechless—I'm doing it."

Finally, a fish appears: "You see him?—I see him!—I don't see him!—He's right there!—Where?—You got him?—I got him!—He's on!—He's off—I've still got him!—He's ripping it!—He's one mad fish!—Man, he's mad!—What a monster!—Stay out of there, you bad boy!—Oh, he's a good boy!—He's sure a good one—We having fun yet?—I got him wore out—He's taking line!—Bonefish never quit!—Cobia don't know the meaning of the word quit—Bluefish are no quitters—Come on, fish!—These fish sure love to fight."

As the battle draws to a close, the dialogue changes tone, depending on whether the angler is fishing with a fly rod versus bait-casting, spinning, or trolling gear. A fishing-show host may be proficient with all kinds of tackle, but he acts more polite with a fly rod in his hands: "What a beauty!—That's a dandy!—Nice fish!—They're all nice—Congratulations!—I learned from a master—Perfect eating size, hun, we'll let this one go—That was great!—Let's find another—That works for me."

In the following scenario, several anglers continue fishing after they've already landed a limit. In the original shows, the action involved lingcod, cobia, and striped bass. In the striper show, previously boated fish were kept "alive" in coolers of sea water while other fish were landed. If one of those stripers was larger than a captive fish, the previously caught fish was thrown back and the freshly caught striper dropped in its place. It the case of the lingcod and cobia, the extra-limit fish were "lip-gaffed" and brought aboard for a photo op before being dropped back over the side: "What you got there, boy?—Look at the size of hint!—Look at the size of that mouth!—Mine's bigger than yours—My fish could eat yours for breakfast!—He's not that small!—He's bait!—Put a hook in him and catch a real fish!—He swallowed the hook—He sure wanted that bait—Think you can get the hook back?—I don't see it—He's bleeding—That's not so bad—We got to keep him—We can't—Just cut the leader—We should keep him—The hook will rust out—The fish will be no worse for wear—There he goes!—See, he's fine—Wash that blood—Give me a high-five!"

Regardless of what species are caught (or how they're caught), all trips end with the same sentiments with which they began: "Unbelievable!—One of the most unique experiences of my life—Really unique!—How could it be any better than this?—It couldn't be any better—I wonder what the poor folks are doing?"

Some outings wrap up with a back-at-the-lodge interview with the resort manager. This was my favorite: "You lived here all your life?—Yep—I bet you've see a lot of changes—Yep— I bet you've seen things a person like me could never imagine—Yep."

While channel surfing, I discovered an angling series apparently inspired by *The Man Show*'s "Girls Jumping on Trampolines." It features three young ladies who'll never fish anywhere they might have to wear more than a bikini. I feel sorry for two of the girls, who seem more genuinely interested in fish and fishing than the "man-handler" who travels with them. (What does that guy do?!) The girls squeal and wiggle whenever a fish is hooked. The two not in the fighting-chair lean over the lass who is to give her words of encouragement and the camera an eyeful. (I didn't take any notes while watching this show, but I did clean my glasses during commercial breaks.)

Well, I see by the Weather Channel there's a storm brewing off Japan, which won't affect the East Coast for at least three weeks. Sounds like a good time for another once-in-a-lifetime, really unique experience on the tuna grounds in my (now) nineteen-foot Whaler.

How could it get any better than this?

5

Mental Health Deflates in Winnebago Sturgeon Shack

Saturday, February 14. A Sturgeon-Spearer's Diary.

4:30 a.m.: Opening morning. Heading north on Highway 45 toward Winnebago with just the stars as my companions. Mentally sharp. Ready. Enthusiastic. I haven't seen a sturgeon in eight years of sturgeon-spearing. Today's the day.

6:30 a.m.: Met my guide, Bill Jenkins in Pipe, Wisconsin, on the east side of Winnebago. Every year I give Bill fifty dollars. He lets me stare down into a hole. Show me a better bargain.

6:45 a.m.: Jim Sullivan of Jefferson gives me a ride out to my one-man shack far out on the ice of Winnebago. Jim's been spearing for a decade, with hundreds of hours staring into the water. He thinks he saw one nine years ago. I'm in the presence of greatness.

7 a.m.: All settled in now, in my six-foot-by-eight-foot shack. The trap door in the floor has been lifted back and I can sit on this folding chair and stare down at a refrigerator-size hole. Above the hole, hanging down from a nail, is a heavy, iron, five-pronged spear with a rope attached, poised to drop when the monster appears. The gas heater has been lit by my guide. It will soon be toasty warm in here.

7:15 a.m.: Fire's out. It's freezing.

7:20 a.m.: It's quiet now, and black. I can see about twelve feet down into the swirling green hues of Winnebago, and if I tilt this notebook just right, I can scribble by that hue almost legibly. At aunt eight feet my guide has suspended my decoy, a two-foot-long white piece of plastic pipe. "What a stupid fish to rise to a piece of PVC pipe," I think as I stare down at a piece of PVC pipe. Unexplained: brief flashback to my beautiful wife, Lori, in a warm bed that I left on a Saturday morning so I could drive up here alone and sit in a cold shack and stare at this pipe. Yep, that's a stupid fish all right.

8:30 a.m.: Well, at least it's warm now. It's been ninety minutes and Mr. Big, no doubt, is just a minute or two from arriving underneath the ice. I'm still mentally sharp.

8:32 a.m.: A bubble just came all the way up. I watched it.

8:33 a.m.: 'Nother one.

8:35 a.m.: John Jenkins, Bill's son and a veteran spearer, just showed up. He has many sturgeons under his belt. He wants this reporter to get one, too. I don't know why, but year after year after year after year after year John wears the same look of pity around me. He gives me his secret weapon decoy. It's . . . and please keep this quiet so everyone's not utilizing it . . . a plastic pail. I thank John profusely as the pail is lowered to hang next to the white pipe. John tells me that Paul Wargowski is on his first sturgeon hunt, his shack just a hundred yards from mine. Old Paul (who's actually only about thirty) flipped back the lid this morning and there was a fifty-eight-inch sturgeon. Just three minutes into his first season, and his tag is filled. I tell John to congratulate good old Paul Wargowski of Whitewater for me, although I don't know him.

8:36 a.m.: John just left. I don't like Paul Wargowski of Whitewater.

8:37 a.m.: I'm humbled, a little emotional as John leaves the shack. I mean, how many guys give you a pail? I make a note to give John a can, or maybe even a bottle someday.

8:46 a.m.: Well no wonder it's a secret weapon. I stare down and the pail is going round and round, twirlly, twirlly, twiirrrllly in the green hues. The pipe just sits there like a lazy pipe. Pull your weight, man, I yell! . . . No reaction.

9:45 a.m.: Twirrlly, twiiirrrllyyy, twwwwiiirrrllly. Still mentally sharp. But I think there may be someone in here.

9:48 a.m.: He's here all right. Somewhere in the dark. Lurking. I'll act unalarmed.

10:30 a.m.: If I stand on my tiptoes, I can just barely squash my hair on the ceiling.

11 a.m.: Discussing things with myself for an hour now. Made unsettling self-discovery— I'm pretty boring. Not good. This shatters my whole self-image. Little wonder I never had a date in high school.

11:30 a.m.: Tried playing one hundred questions about my life. Only missed seven. Self-esteem rising again.

11:37 a.m.: Just checked my notes. Twenty-seven pages of "all work and no play makes Dick a dull boy." What does that mean? That guy in the shack is messing with me.

11:45 a.m.: It is indeed toasty warm in here. I'm down to my T-shirt, sweating. There's a fly climbing up the wall. Yea, right. In February. In Wisconsin. Like that's not a "plant." Now I know someone is in here, watching, watching, watching me. Watching me to see if I kill the fly. To see if I'm sane. I saw *Psycho*. Norman Bates. Dressed in his mother's clothes. He wouldn't kill the fly either. He knew "they" were watching, too. I'll wait this thing out. I will not touch that fly.

11:55 a.m.: It's a bit hot. Should have worn Lori's skirt. That short, black leather number.

NOON: Just smashed the fly with the spear. I knew they were watching. A siren just went off.

12:30 p.m.: Bill Jenkins is here. Spearing's over for the day. Bill wants to know why I look so flushed. He pries my fingers off the spear handle. "Dick . . . Dick . . . Are you all right?" I hear his distant voice. "Am I all right?" I hear my answer: "Am I all right? I will be—just as soon as you sign me up for next year."

6

Sample Fisherman's Prenuptial Agreement

WHEREAS the groom has accumulated prior to marriage an invaluable supply of fishing rods, the bride waives all claims to both the joint ownership and usage of same. On specially designated occasions, the groom may allow limited use of same but no post-marital rights belong to any in-laws.

WHEREAS the groom has fully disclosed to the bride-to-be the approximate present value of his fishing equipment, it is possible that something was missed, and her wedding party shall not be able to claim ownership or lease rights in a separate party agreement.

WHEREAS the groom's ability to enjoy fishing entails understanding the most current technological advances and the use of the most advanced equipment and techniques, the groom has both the right to freely dispose of older equipment to make room for the new and/or simply add property that becomes his single estate.

WHEREAS the groom will grant a special dispensation to allow the bride to handle the equipment in the normal spring-housecleaning activities. It is further provided that should a fishing emergency arise, small dowry items may be pawned without advance notice until such times that the groom can concentrate on recovering same.

WHEREAS in the event of the death of the groom, the last will and testament will carry instructions that mandate the joint burial of the man and his equipment. It is further provided that the grave location is kept from the wedding party and, if necessary, a restraining order be filed against any remaining shovel-toting brothers-in-law.

Therefore and there now, in consideration of the mutual promises and agreements set forth therein and forever there more, both parties agree that any balance of taxes owed by the groom becomes a joint responsibility of the bride and her wedding party. This agreement is made in the state where the groom is a resident fisherman and shall be construed, governed, and interpreted in accordance with the laws of the Commonwealth or the Department of Fish and Game, depending on the season.

· 7 ·

Fishing Quiz Show

Circle T for True or F for False.

The best time to catch farmed fish is after the hatchery manager goes home. T or F

Catfish whiskers are heavier at the end of the day. A five-blade razor is recommended. T or F

According to the latest papal announcements, fishing is no longer a sin if accompanied by a 5 percent increase in tithing or your wife going off the pill. T or F

Fishing rods are now available by species: walleye, bass, etc. They all look much alike and will snag carp, bullheads, and other jetsam and flotsam with equal ease. T or F

One inch of slushy ice should be thick enough to support your mother-in-law. T or F

California law requires the use of rubber-tipped arrows while bowfishing for snorkelers. T or F

If you need spousal hair to complete a hand-tied fly, wait until they are asleep or passed out. T or F

Fly-fishing "widows" are as easy to pick up as bass-fishing "widows." Mind you, wine is generally more expensive than beer. T or F

Tournament fishermen use slip knots when tying and then anchoring a large bass to an undisclosed water location. T or F

To think like a fish, you must drink like one. T or F

*Compiler's note: Winners will be announced in the hardcover edition of this book and be given a ticket for a drawing for a Hemingway Classic 20 In-Shore Fishing Boat or reasonable desktop facsimile depending on net proceeds of the first paperback edition.

IF THE WHEEL HAD NEVER BEEN INVENTED

• 8 •

Explosives

The game warden had been hearing a report about a backwoods character who had been bringing a tubful of fish home every time he went out. So, curious and suspicious, the warden asked and was welcomed to tag along on his next fishing trip.

The game warden met the fisherman at a small lake early the next morning and both set out on the lake. He did, however, notice that the fisherman didn't have a fishing pole in his boat, just an old tackle box and a large net. Once they got out to a certain spot on the lake, the fisherman cut the motor and reached into the tackle box. He pulled out a stick of dynamite, lit it, and tossed it into the lake. As soon as it blew up, a large number of fish floated to the top and the fisherman started dipping his net in the water to retrieve his "catch" of the day.

The game warden came unglued: "You can't do that; it's against the law." The old fisherman didn't respond. He just reached into the tackle box, pulled out another stick of dynamite, and then threw it into the game warden's lap, saying with a smile, "Are you just going to sit and talk or are we going to fish?"

Dedicated to the "M–79 Ka Boom" fishermen along the Vàm Cỏ Đông River, RVN 1967.

9

Golden Oldies

Compiler's Note: You may have already heard these oldies but goodies, but we have leftover blank space.

Two fishermen were discussing their catch the previous day, and one said he's caught a salmon that weighed in at two hundred pounds.

"Two hundred pounds!" exclaimed the other man. "You and I know that salmon don't get that big!"

"You may think that, but my fish weighed that much. Tell me, what did you catch?"

"Had a no-fish day, but I hooked an old lamp with markings on the bottom that read 'Property of Christopher Columbus 1492.' The oddest thing about the lamp was a candle inside that was still lit."

"Tell you what," the salmon fisherman said. "You blow out that damned candle and I'll knock off a hundred and fifty pounds."

Ole and Sven rented a boat and were catching a lot of fish.

Sven said, "This is such a great spot. Let's mark it so we can find it again."

Ole said, "Okay," and started to put a mark on the side of the boat.

Sven said, "Hey, Ole, what are you doing?"

Ole replied, "Marking the spot."

"Don't be stupid, Ole," Sven said. "What if we don't get the same boat next time?"

Rental boat manager on megaphone: "Boat number 99, return to the dock immediately or I'll have to charge you overtime."

Boat hand: "Hey boss, there is no boat number 99. We only have seventy-five boats."

Rental boat manager: "Boat number 66, are you in trouble?"

While driving alongside a creek, a motorist came across a young fellow lazing under a tree with a fishing line in the water. The cork was bobbing frantically.

"Hey," said the motorist, "you've got a bite."

"Yeah," the fisherman drawled. "Would you mind pulling it out?"

The motorist did so, only to have the lazy fisherman ask, "Would you mind taking it off the hook, re-baiting the hook, and tossing my line back in the creek?"

This was done and the motorist commented jokingly, "Being as lazy as you are, you ought to have some kids to do these things for you."

"Not a bad idea," yawned the fisherman. "Got any ideas where I can find a pregnant woman?"

One day when Lars and Sven are fishing, a hearse crosses the bridge nearby. Lars takes off his hat and places it over his heart until the funeral service passes by.

Sven looks at Lars and says, "I'm, surprised, Lars, that you were so respectful."

Lars replies, "It's the least I could do. I was married to her for thirty years."

OR

When his wife of fifty years died suddenly, the old fisherman didn't cry. He didn't even tear up at her funeral service. Later in the local tavern he was having a beer when his fishing buddy asked how he was holding up. "Oh, I'm doing fine," he said. "It isn't as if she was a blood relative."

BAIT TRIFECTA

A guy goes to work one day and says to his good friend, "This is confidential: My wife has worms."

His friend says "Yikes! That sounds serious."

The guy responds, "No, not really. You know how much I like to fish."

Several years ago, a local man went ice fishing, stepped on thin ice, and fell through. That was the last anyone had heard about him until the following spring, when his wife received a telegram from the chief of police of a small village downriver. The telegram read: Your husband's body found STOP in very bad condition and full of eels STOP send instruction STOP

The bereaved widow rushed to the telegraph office and sent the following directive: Sell eels STOP Send proceeds STOP Set him again STOP.

An old fellow from Maine goes lobster fishing and his wife falls overboard, goes under, and doesn't come back up. He waits a while and finally goes back to shore.

The next day, another fisherman pulls up to the dock and says to the old fellow, "I got your wife caught in one of my traps with lobsters stuck to her. What should I do?"

The lobsterman says, "Well, give me half the lobsters and let's set her up again."

One Saturday morning, Henry gets up early, quietly dresses and makes a quick lunch, grabs his gear, and heads out to the garage to hook up the boat. As he opens the garage door, he sees a rainy, cold day ahead. It's not just rain; sleet is mixed in with a stiff wind from the north. He thinks of a day in this weather and goes back in the house for a quick check of the weather channel.

With their gloomy forecast, an easy decision is reached. He brings his stuff back into the house, quietly undresses, and slips back into bed. He cuddles up to his wife, thinking maybe a warm reception, and whispers, "It's really crummy weather out there today."

To which she sleepily replies, "Yeah, can you believe my dumb husband is out fishing in it?"

Lutefisk

Compiler's note: You may wonder why a Scandinavian American holiday fish dish is included in a humor collection. You may still wonder why after reading this section.

Definition: A chemically altered codfish, "lutefisk" (or "lye fish") refers to a fish that has been salted and dried. Originally skinned, boned, and soaked (or "luted") in lye for ten days, or however long it takes for big Ole to put on his winter long johns, then rinsed for almost a week to "cure" the meat. Too much lye and the fish get as mushy as Swedish meatballs or Finnish resolve to dance when the music starts. Too little and the thicker parts aren't done, which in the world of fine lutefisk dining means nothing.

Lutefisk is cooked by baking, boiling, or steaming. Wrapped in cheesecloth or Big Ole's tighty-whities, the flesh is dropped in hot water and then removed to steam dry and flake. Lutefisk is never cooked in an aluminum pot as it will turn the inner lining black, so you can imagine what a serving will do to your stomach lining. Halfway through the cooking, in very hot, steamy church or lodge kitchens, Finnish housewives flog the chefs with pine boughs. In the dining area, young family members cough a required taste into a napkin and others hope the kitchen runs out of this entrée. Older generations burp out a "Yah, you betcha, it was good as last year's."

In traditional Scandinavian American households, lutefisk cooking is taught to the next generation, who have sworn on a plate of lefse that as soon as Dad starts "forgetting" the good old days, the imaginary home country, they will misplace the recipe for this holiday dish and serve Swedish meatballs from IKEA. Lutefisk will, however, continue to be served at the senior home to those who appreciate any hot, soft meal.

Lutefisk: It Will Put the Fear of Cod in You.
May Your Lutefisk Be Flakier Than Your Friends.

A sample verse of one variation of the "Song of Lutefisk" set to the music of "O Tannenbaum" in Sons of Norway Lodges.

> O Lutefisk, O Lutefisk,
> I put you in the doorway
> O Lutefisk, O Lutefisk,
> To ripen you like they do in Norway
> I put you in the avenue
> A dog came by and sprinkled you
> I hit it with my overshoe
> And held my nose while eating you

Cooking instructions

1. Lay the lutefisk on a pine board.
2. Flatten with a heavy object.
3. Season with salt and pepper.
4. Bake fish on the board for 30 minutes.
5. Remove from oven and let cool.
6. Discard fish and eat the board.

Variation: add melted butter or a white sauce before serving board.

Is the taste of lutefisk, as described by John Louis Andersons in his Scandinavian *Humor and Other Myths*, "like dishtowels soaked in fish sweat or lumpy cod-liver-oil flavored Jell-O?" Served with Ufda family flair, your ordinary senses will excuse themselves for the powder room, and umami is already asking the valet for the car keys.

Two fellows are standing out in front of the general store when one points to the other's dog and speaks. "Look Lars, your dog must have worms because he's licking his ass."

And Lars says, "No, Ole, he's been eating lutefisk, and he's trying to get the taste out of his mouth."

· *11* ·

Forecasts

$\mathcal{F}$ishermen share with hunters a need to predict success, estimates that reach beyond the accuracy of the bumpkin on the porch who nods off with "Ya shoulda been here last week!"

Anthropologists have been fishing for any secrets, patterns, or cycles of successful subsistence fishermen. Different tribes, including the Maori of New Zealand and bachelor farmers of northern Minnesota, have been interviewed but with little success. One correlation that is commonly accepted is the position of the moon and the best times to catch fish. This system claims that more fish are caught plus or minus two hours of the moon being directly overhead on the days around the new moon phase. Next best time, say the Moonies, is plus or minus one and a half hours of being straight overhead near the dates of the full moon. The best fishing hours during the moon's first and third quarters are not so good. If all this makes sense, please thank the publisher.

Another forecasting system is the solar/lunar columns found in the front of fishing magazines. These forecasts are described by day and date and should not be shown to anyone dependent on your fishing success (spouses in particular). The only dates omitted are the national and personal holidays. The former works best for civil-service employees who can stretch three-day holidays into a lifetime of mixed service; for your beloved, it can be predicted that no matter how successful you are on your wedding anniversary it won't make any difference.

Another way to forecast fishing is to predict the tides. Tide, for all you flatlanders, is the vertical rise and fall of water, not laundry detergent. Tides carry bait fish to predators. There are generally two high and two low tides every day to the last day of your life. Given variations

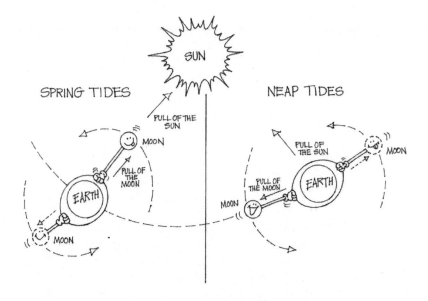

in each tide and since the moon is the stronger source of gravity, tides follow a lunar day (which is fifty minutes longer than a solar day), making tomorrow's tides fifty minutes (or sixteen hectares in Canada) later than today's. Today is yesterday's tomorrow.

If the sun and the moon are in alignment, as in a new or full moon, spring tides will occur with higher highs and lower lows and strong currents. Neap tides occur at quarter moons with the sun and moon at right angles in the house of Aquarius. Neap tides are the reverse of spring tides. Other influences on tide are winds and barometric pressure: with an onshore wind and dropping barometric pressure, the tides will be higher. Again, the reverse applies. It is also during this time that the PMS tables occur, and the high percentage of water in a woman's body follows the ocean movements. During spring tides, women will leave the home to look for a better-paying job and ask you to take out the garbage more often.

If you are fishing nontidal lakes with a storm moving in and the barometer dropping, good fishing can be expected, but let your brother-in-law carry the steel fishing rod. Fishing in the rain can go either way; it depends more on how wet you want to get. (The fish feel they are wet enough.) Cloudy days reduce light penetration into the water, making fish feel safer—that's why they are fish and not U-boat commanders.

The worst forecast is cold, clear weather following a storm; fish would rather join you in front of the TV while you watch the bowl games.

If all this empirical information still doesn't make you a believer, rely on superstition. Like anyone dealing with blind forces and luck, fishermen rely on fables and fibs. No matter how thick your polarizing glasses, the water cannot be read with any certainty, and that's why famous dowsers like F. Kohler, owner of the Celestial Marine Junkyard and famous bottom-rock fisherman, collect and analyze fishing myths. It is Professor Kohler's opinion that fishermen don't necessarily have to experience several events to provide a base for a particular superstition; furthermore, most fishermen don't even need a complete event to fix on a logical construct for why they are or are not catching fish.

The more popular grouping of superstitions deals with weather:

> Red lips at night, clear skin in the morning
> Wind from the north, stay in port
> Wind from the east, fishing's least
> Wind from the south, fish open their mouth
> Wind from the west, fishing's best
> Wind from the bow, your brother-in-law's back

Adults Only

KEEP THESE UNDER YOUR HAT

Liam and Finn are out fishing, and the boat's motor quits. Liam says to Finn, "What are we going to do now?"

Finn replies, "We'll just have to wait for help."

After a couple days, they are still miles from the coast and come across a bottle. Liam opens the bottle and out pops a genie who offers to grant them one wish. Quick as a wink, Liam says, "Turn the sea into Guinness!" and immediately the sea is black with Guinness.

Finn says, "You stupid fool! Now we'll have to piss in the boat!"

Henry had driven by a lake several times and noticed other anglers, so he decided to try his luck in this new spot. On his first day, he didn't catch a thing but noticed another fisherman was catching them hand over fist. He had to learn his secret.

"Pardon me, sir, but what kind of bait are you using?"

The other man looked a little sheepish and said, "Well, I'm a surgeon and was surprised to learn tonsils work really well."

Henry thought about it a bit and decided to change his tactic the next day. The next morning, he still had no luck, but another guy was also just killing it.

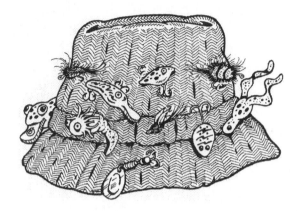

"Excuse me, sir, but I need some advice on bait. I'm not having any luck at all."

"Well, I could, but my advice won't do you any good because I'm using human appendixes today."

Henry thought, well, would come back. He really had to make a change and come back the next day for one last try. The third day, Henry again had no luck but ended up standing close to yet another angler who was outfishing everyone. He had to confirm the very best bait.

"Excuse me, sir, are you also a doctor?"

"No," replied the man, "I am a rabbi."

There once was an old guy who lost his long-time fishing partner and decided to ask the young guy down the street if he'd like to go fishing with him. The old guy says, "Sure," he would like to go sometime, and the old guy says, "Okay, how about this Saturday?" The young guy says, "Sure, what time? The old timer says, "Five a.m.," and the younger says, "Okay . . . but I might be late."

At 5 a.m. on Saturday, the young guy shows up and off to the lake the two go. When they get there, the younger guy says, "Can I fish off the left side of the boat?" The old guy has no reason not to let him fish off that side and says, "Sure." As the day goes by, the young man catches fish after fish after fish on the left side of the boat while the old guy catches just a few.

When they get home, the old guy asks the young guy if he wants to go again next Saturday. The young fellow says, "Sure," and asks what time. The old guy again says, "5 a.m.," and the young fellow says, "Okay, but I might be late."

On the following Saturday, the young guy shows up on time and off they go. When they get to the lake, the younger guy asks if he can fish off the right side of the boat. The old guy agrees and as the day goes on, the youngster catches fish after fish after fish, while the old guy catches just a few. This really gets the old guy and finally he must ask.

"What's up with all this, you might be late, but you aren't, and you have to fish out of a certain side of the boat and then you catch all the fish?"

The young guy explains that when he wakes up in the morning to go fishing, he looks at his wife sleeping next to him. If she is on her left side, he knows to fish off the left side of the boat. If she is sleeping on her right side, he knows to fish off the right side of the boat.

The old man asks, "Well, what if she is sleeping on her back?"

The young man replies, ". . . Then I will be late."

• *13* •

How to Boat or Beach a Fish

$\mathcal{A}$fter bringing the fish to its almost final end, you have to decide whether to listen to the nattering nabobs about catch and release or just keep the fish, like the good book tells you.

HOW TO BOAT A FISH: Gaffs are stage hooks with sharper points and are indications to a fish that you want their shiny hide hanging on the family room wall. Hook the fish in the jaw and flip aboard. If it's a large, long fish, reach across and over with two gaffs, spaced evenly along the length and roll into the boat.

The most popular method of *boating* a smaller fish is to use your bare hands. Put your thumb on its lower lip and force its jaw back as you lift the fish out of the water. Research on the lower jaws of bass shows that the excessive strain can damage joints, causing names for released fish, like Old Slackjaw, to be coined. Don't try this technique on the larger billfish without a good pair of gloves.

If you decide against all advice to use a gun and just blast a hole in that five-hundred-pound halibut that refuses to come to Papa, remember that bullets can skip on water: Shoot true. And don't shoot the monster one more time for good measure once it's on the boat unless it's not your boat. Since fish don't heal well from gunshot wounds, this practice is not often used in catch and release.

HOW TO BEACH A FISH: If you don't have any line left or don't want to use any line at all, a properly hooked fish will beach easily if you run directly and swiftly away from the line of retrieve, pulling the fish ashore. (Stop running when you've reached the porch, if not before.) If you drag the fish for a short distance on the shore, the effort will shorten your scaling time.

31

If you are on a boat, you can do the same thing by holding the rod out toward shore and running the craft as close to camp as possible. If it's a big fish, drive the boat right onto the trailer and have a friend pull the entire rig and tackle out of the water.

If you can't boat the fish, tow it by tying a tail rope to the stern cleat with its mouth roped shut. Understand that's how Hemingway's Old Man lost his fish, but then again, that book is fiction. If it's a real big fish, tow it alongside so skunked fishermen (losers!) can't harpoon it. Don't run up the fishing flat until your brother-in-law, on shore, can see it.

· *14* ·

The Marshmallow Purists

*M*aybe it's the fact that we are away from home and are overcome by the joyous anticipation of adventure. Or maybe it's because we can't resist the urge to redefine our identity in the presence of those who don't know us. Or perhaps it's just that, regardless of age, we are all still kids full of barely contained devilment. Whatever the reason, I have observed that the practical joke is never more tempting than when we gather with new companions to share our common obsession with fishing or hunting in distant places. The most even-tempered among us is very likely to become either predator or prey.

My friend Matt Hodgson, for example, pursues his ruling passion for fishing seriously. But like many who have been at it for a long time, he sometimes grows weary of the near-religious pedantry and politically correct intolerance that he encounters among some anglers who have been newly baptized in the oft-contrived rituals of this sport. "It gets tedious," he observed as he told me this story.

On a recent trip to fish the Yellowstone River in Montana, he and his companions found themselves one morning in the company of a guide who seemed far too inclined to preach the gospel. "Now, I don't know how you fellows fish back home," he sniffed, "but here we fish only with flies and we release all trout. I would much prefer that you fish with dry flies, but if you have some other notions, we should discuss them."

Matt had hardly anticipated such a sermon. Not only is he unlikely to be taken for a rube, but his experience as a fly fisherman and fly tier far exceeded the guide's.

"Well, to tell the truth," Matt replied, "what I had in mind was a technique we prefer back home in North Carolina. Why don't you fellows go on ahead, and I'll run back into town and get about two hundred yards of stout cord and some 3/0 hooks. This looks like a really good place to set a trotline. You don't right offhand know where I could get a mess of chicken necks for bait, do you?"

Sometimes the best way to crush a stereotype is to play to your adversary's worst fears. For a moment, the guide looked as though he had caught a bullet with his teeth, but when the laughter died down and he realized that Matt had no intention of stringing chicken necks across the Yellowstone, he relaxed and joined his peers for an enjoyable day of fly fishing.

Those of us born and bred in the briar patch of Southern culture are frequently called upon to diffuse an unfortunate (or fortunate) stereotype when we travel to distant lands where our mother tongue is automatically linked with toothless ignorance and inbreeding. But sometimes it's fun to keep those suspicions alive, too.

In the late 1970s, some friends and I journeyed to Pennsylvania to fish the storied limestone streams where Vincent Marinaro, Charley Fox, Ed Koch, and others had spawned a new and highly sophisticated technique for catching wild trout on flies, carefully fashioned to imitate terrestrial insects. We had spent the winter tying flies, reading the literature, and preparing ourselves for this crusade to Mecca.

We drove all night and rendezvoused with our Keystone-State guides on the stream shortly after dawn. They seemed a bit reserved, but they looked at our tackle and apparently decided that we, at least, looked like fly fisherpeople. My friends, however, were not about to let such an educational opportunity pass.

As we tromped down to the water, we swapped those precious bits of information that are thinly disguised to reveal our knowledge and establish our credentials. Fly boxes were shared and patterns compared. Just then it looked as though we might be accepted, because one of the Pennsylvania anglers asked to see the patterns I'd been tying for this occasion.

Proudly, I produced my fly box and flipped open the lid. Each compartment was filled with tiny marshmallows, sorted by color—white, pink, yellow, and green. I was stunned. The Pennsylvanians looked like someone had slapped them with a wet carp.

"But . . . but," I stammered.

"Yep," said one of my North Carolina companions. "We should have warned you, I suppose. Dean, here, can match any hatch with a marshmallow. Fishes them dry, too."

The worst of it was that my Tar Heel buddies had emptied my several hundred flies into a paper sack—it took hours to get them sorted out. But everyone—well, almost everyone—had a good laugh and another stereotype had bitten the dust. We had a grand time fishing together that week.

And one of us had colorful snacks to eat on the stream, too.

15

Fish Biology 101

WHAT IS A FISH?

In Webster's view, it doesn't take much to be a fish—just be any one of the three classes of cold bloods living in water and have permanent gills for breathing, fins, and, to be a "real" fish, scales. The *jaw-less* fish family has but two American members, the hagfish and lamprey. The weak backboned *cartilaginous* family includes sharks and rays. The bony fish family contains many of our friends and is the subject of this book. But, outside of ichthyologists, Buck wants you to know that the entire fish group is receiving a bum rap.

The trouble is indicated in our language. If you drink like a fish, you shouldn't! If something is fishy, it's highly suspect. A fish story is a fable fabricated while you pull up the driveway. Corporate career women are unfairly described as barracuda (especially when there is a much wider range of predators to choose from). For those who read good mysteries, red herrings are false clues. Wrapped up in a newspaper, a dead mackerel is an important part of Italian communications.

Why aren't there any good nursery rhymes about fish? "Fishy, fishy in the brook, come bite my hook" doesn't count. It's no accident that with a matriarch like Mother Goose, storybooks are full of pithy little pieces about ducks, ganders, and other cuddly non-fish things. Within her limited purview, she's probably witnessed a largemouth bass dining on duckling now and then, but that's no reason to exclude the entire clan. Have you also noticed the small animals selected to represent the dominant values of high schools, colleges, and companies on athletic playing fields? Not everybody can be a cougar or bobcat. Just to avoid the *fish* subject, team managers have even resorted to naming their unruly, overpaid mobs by the color of their socks.

The animal world understands the importance of fish. There isn't a dog of good breeding alive that doesn't want to roll on the ground with a decaying carp carcass. Where lives a cat that doesn't prefer a fresh slab of fish flesh over canned commercial mush? Seagulls need fish to reload their bombing compartments. Grizzlies love to chomp on big salmon, and nature societies love to put the bite on the wealthy for these photo opportunities.

This paean could go on forever, but there are other fish to fry.

Outside Parts of a Fish

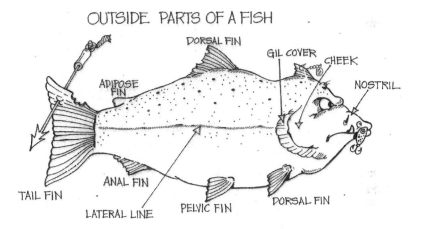

OUTSIDE PARTS OF A FISH

DORSAL FIN

GIL COVER

CHEEK

ADIPOSE FIN

NOSTRIL

ANAL FIN

TAIL FIN

LATERAL LINE

PELVIC FIN

DORSAL FIN

What a Fish Looks Like

All fish have common characteristics, with freshwater fish varying only slightly from saltwater fish. The principal differences are between what you see on the outside and the horrors within.

Fins: The tail or caudal fin is used for turbo propulsion and steering. When a fish is being retrieved, the tail fin is used as drag.

The anal fin is named after its strategic location near the "back door." It is frequently used to wave away embarrassing gas bubbles.

The pelvic fin props a fish at rest on the bottom and are used by slower fish to wave on passing predators. Etiquette requires that fish pass or overtake one another only on the left side.

The pectoral fin when waved invites friendly social intercourse.

The dorsal fins are what shark imitators use to break the surface water and give fear to bathers. The forward spiny fin is used to impale troublesome neighbors and the trailing soft fin assists locomotion.

The adipose fin is an indication of the inbreeding endemic to hatchery fish, similar to the seminal tails of the royal families of Europe.

Gill cover: Where all the gills are stored for safekeeping.

Other outside body parts: Include nostrils, cheeks, and, yes, lips, which can be easily ripped off by an anxious fisherman.

Inside Parts of a Fish

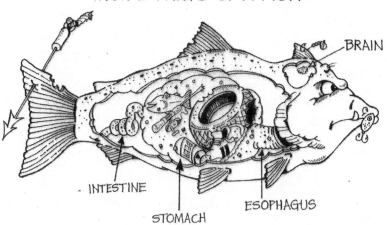

The fish brain is located high in the cranial cavity and seldom used. Fish psychologists have tried to monitor fish brain waves for any evidence of species identity and self-esteem, but unfortunately for fish-rights activists, the brain waves indicate only a slavish weakness for easy food.

The guts of the matter focus on the passages—from the mouth through the esophagus, to temporary residence in the stomach, and finally power flushing via the intestinal sewer pipe. A full stomach of garbage will conceal organs pushed out of their traditional hiding spots: the heart, home of all romantic fish notions and broken only when a fly fisherman forgets to smooch his fish before release; the liver, an over-worked poison fighter; the kidneys, pushing water into water; the gas bladder, for setting the proper depth levels; and the sex organs, which are too exaggerated to be included in a guidebook read by the whole family.

SENSES

Hearing

Fish have inner ears that isolate and identify sounds. These inner ears are found inside the skull, one each behind the eyes, and contain three semicircular canals and three ear stones that rattle about the not-quite-full cranial cavity. The "stones" are covered by sensory hair cells, and sound waves move tiny bones called "otoliths" to stimulate the hair cells, which send complicated messages to a brain preoccupied with that awful smell upstream.

Researchers estimate that fish can hear sound waves in the range of 20 to 1,000 hertz or cycles per second, about twice the range heard by a fisherman listening closely to his wife. With water five times denser than air, sound travels about five times faster. Quiet, please!

Sight

Few fish are as blind as the batfish, and most have good eyesight. Evolution has played a large part in the particulars of eye placement. For example, the two eyes on the same side of a halibut or flounder resulted from the constant irritation to the downside eye of these bottom feeders, and somewhere along the evolutionary trail, the bottom eye was persuaded to join its buddy topside. As the fish matures, the eye moves from either the right- or left-hand side, whichever is dominant. Fish ophthalmologists are complaining that since the top eye doesn't have to work so hard anymore, signs of "lazy eye" have appeared and crossed eyes are reported.

The fish eye sits in a hard socket with a film-like covering. Without a discernible lid, it's nigh impossible to tell what they might be doing or thinking. They may be just playing dead.

Of importance to the sport fisherman, fish are not colorblind. In clear, bright water, bass can recognize all the season's new colors of lures; while others with more sensitive peepers (like walleyes) can distinguish only particular colors (in their case, orange). Water filters out color the deeper you go, making brightness and movement more important. How far fish can see depends on the clarity of the water, with an average between fifteen and twenty-five feet. Predators have very good eyesight and stand a good chance of catching three square meals a day.

Fish can see sportsmen standing along the edge of a riverbank. If an angler stoops below an angle of ten degrees from the point on the water surface directly above the fish, the fish will just see the fishing rod held on high. You will not be seen if you are five feet tall and thirty feet away from the fish. If you have to get closer, crouch or crawl carefully and wear clothing that makes you look like a bush. It's one of the rare occasions in life when it pays to be short. Most fly fishermen are shorter or seem more diminutive than bait-crankers.

If you are saltwater fishing, the fish will jump out of the water to try to get a good look. The real big game fish tend to be a little farsighted, and it won't be until you lean over the side of the boat for a gaffing that the fish will get a better look at you. It's at that point that the fish may decide not to care anymore.

If a fish does see you, your fishing isn't necessarily over. And if you block the sun for a baked trout struggling over a shallow riverbed, the fish may return the favor by taking a less-than-perfect imitation from a boob in waders. Young fish have short memories and old fish lose theirs. The really old fish forget why they are in the water in the first place.

Taste

While we humans have taste buds in only our mouths, fish can have them most anywhere. Catfish have taste buds in their whiskers and on their fins, as well as on their lips and inside their mouths. When a cell of a bud senses a chemical substance, a message goes to their tiny brains to be interpreted as good to eat or not. For example, bass buds guide them to chomp into a tasty frog and reject a nasty toad. The ever-surprising catfish can "taste" rotten chicken guts a long ways off. The most sensitive buds can enjoy "taste" without even eating, but these buds belong only to the haughtiest fish-food critics.

Most fish will "mouth" a lure or bait to taste it, and that leads to many an innocent downfall. Many artificial bait manufacturers are adding salt, a mineral that is released when one fish bites another. A popular lure is salted in brine pork rind; fish living near state parks prefer the pork-rind lures, especially if there aren't enough Fritos to go around.

Smell

Fish olfactory organs are in much the same place as yours, below the eyes and above the mouth. Their four nostrils (*naves*) lead to cavities filled with sensory nerves that are connected to the brain.

Some fish have folds, or *lamellae*, that greatly increase the surface and acuity of their snouts. The larger the nose, the better it can smell you with.

The simple act of breathing compresses the inner "pouch" of fish noses and forces water in and out of the nostrils by the movement of cilia as water washes in the anterior nave and out the posterior, or as water deflects over the olfactory organ while swimming. The olfactory organ sends electrical nerve impulses to the smell center of the brain where they are interpreted. The sense of smell develops as a fish matures.

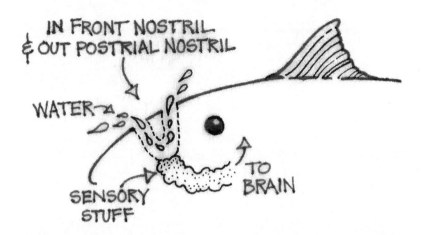

IN FRONT NOSTRIL
& OUT POSTRIAL NOSTRIL

WATER

SENSORY STUFF

TO BRAIN

Early salmon studies showed that fish are repelled by human scent; first by the smell of commercial fishermen; secondly, the smell of the cannery workers who would stuff them into a ten-pound can, and thirdly the Catholics who created the demand. It was shown at the time that fish also avoided smells of bear paws, sea lions, and cracker-crumb breading.

Each fish species has its distinctive odor, and smell helps a fish locate its own school, identify bait-fish for food, or alert it to a predator. Threatened or injured fish release "cold sweat" substances. Scientists theorize that each species releases chemicals to cause specific reactions—courting, spawning, and social order. Female fish exude "perfumes" to start recreational foreplay. There is no concrete evidence that gastric distress can create methane buildup in lower intestines of fish, but this theory may help explain why some fish are always swimming alone.

The Lateral Line

This fish sense falls somewhere between feeling and hearing and is described most accurately in songs by Barry Manilow. The lateral line is a row of sensory organs that run roughly midway along the side of a fish and is sensitive to vibrations and pressure waves. On most fish, the line is easy to identify as it is darker than the rest of the fish. On others, just trust Buck—it's there. Scales near the line have small holes that lead to an underskin canal where all the sensory organs are located and where a

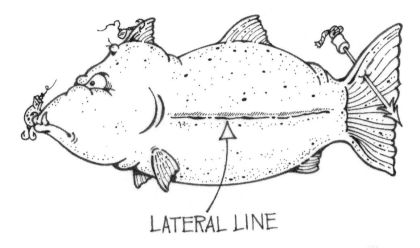

LATERAL LINE

few fish sexologists have positioned the "L" spot. Some fish experts say the line we are able to see is only a portion of the row of sensory organs that extend into the head.

The lateral line serves as an early warning system to detect predators or the buffet line.

It's further speculated that as fish movements create and measure vibrations against stationary objects with these organs, they are able to select and become masters of their habitat. It's not known if they can roll over on their side to mark boats hanging above them in the water.

16

Six Knots for Fly Fishing

*L*ike everything else, fly fishermen need two more knots than necessary. Quickly, it goes like this: The backing is connected to the reel (slipknot), the hip bone is connected to the shoulder bone (oops), the fly line is connected to the leader (nail knot), the leader is connected to the tippet (blood knot), and that's the way of the Lord. Dem flies, dem flies, dem dry flies.

ALBRIGHT KNOT: Reverse spider hitch—best tied with a mirror, or reflection off a chalk stream.

BIMINI TWIST: A double-line knot used for offshore trolling or making a "shock" tippet. Double end of line four feet and twist twenty times, pull ends to tighten. Wind back end tightly and make overhand knot around side of loop. Repeat on other side of loop. Wind line end three times around mid-large loop and pull end through small loop just made. Pull line and large loop tight. Add two shots of tequila for a Jiminy Bimini Twist.

BLOOD KNOT: Ancient ceremony knot that ties two fly fishermen to a promise not to tell bass fishermen how little fun they are really having, usually between two fly-fishing leaders of different moral strengths, a father/son relationship in many cases.

DOUBLE-LOOP CLINCH KNOT: Used to attach a fly to a shock leader. It's a cinch. Just try it. Thatta boy.

NAIL KNOT: For joining fly line and leader butt, this knot is used by fishermen who can't get the hang of other knots. Just do slightly different from Bimini twist.

SPIDER HITCH: Similar in purpose to the Bimini but quicker to tie and easier with only one intoxicated person. Wrap double line five times around thumb and pass large loop through small reverse loop, loopedy, loop. Hold it, my finger is in there. Now, pull tight.

17

Bragging Rights

$\mathcal{F}$ishing is one of the few sport activities that doesn't require or even foster honesty. As one wag put it, honesty is as important in fishing as it is in golf. Nobody expects the whole, nothing-but-the-truth from amateurs when tournament professionals are caught stuffing lead weights in the craw of their daily catch. But fish stories must be told, and the hot air rising from fishing docks, lake taverns, and fishing lodges competes with methane from large cattle feedlots.

THE MORE INNOCENT PAST

"If fishermen only talked about the fish they actually caught, the silence would be unbearable."

Bragging, of course, is in the number or size of the fish or combination thereof. Catch and release, especially with today's enforced slot limits,

AT LUNENBURG, N. S., CANADA

Saw a fair-sized trout here today

One of the Small Ones

relieve the fisherman of actual proof of fish they caught. A musky fisherman could easily say his last fish was so long that he dislocated his shoulder just describing his catch. Fishing conditions can be thrown in, too. "The water in the lake was so low, my boat stopped leaking." When it comes to a large number caught one day, a most honest, humble description by a famed fly fisherman might be, "I caught thirty-six inches of trout today—in six installments."

The boasts of today, however, are lightweight when compared to the tall tales of our pioneers.

An early settler was fishing and ran out of bait. He looked around for a frog or something suitable but couldn't find a thing—until he ran across a little garter snake crawling along with a frog in its mouth. Headed home with supper, I guess. Well, the fisherman caught the snake and took the frog away from him. He put it on the hook and tossed his line out into the water and settled back for a nice afternoon of fishing.

Later, he happened to glance over at the snake and found him just lying there, obviously brokenhearted at the loss of the frog. So the kindhearted fisherman picked up the snake and poured a little of his whisky down the snake's throat, as a sort of pick-me-up. The snake wiggled off, clearly feeling much better, and the fisherman went back to his work.

About fifteen minutes later, the fisherman felt something rubbing up against his ankle, and he looked down to find the little snake with another frog in its mouth.

An angler hooked a perch one morning while fishing in the Platte River. He played the fish all day but was unable to land it. He moored it to the bank with his line and went home to rest. After a good night's sleep, he returned to his task, but still was unable to land the monster.

Days went by in this routine, until finally he hauled it ashore. He dragged it home, but its weight was so great, he sank to his knees on the pavement at every step as he tugged his prize.

The fish was so large he was unable to kill it. He kept it alive in a huge tank he had constructed and removed fillets from its flanks as needed for the table. Eventually he moved back East and on leaving, gave the fish to a widow. She wrote him from time to time, in pursuing years, saying she had gradually sliced to where "the fillets are getting right good." She told the angler the perch often asked about him.

"I caught a trout so large, the picture of it was over three pounds. The negative alone weighed a pound. We just ate in the lake rather than bring it home."

How to Turn a Perfectly Normal Child into a Fisherman

*S*everal years ago, I was consulted by a highly agitated mother who felt something dreadful was happening to her son. "A fatal disease?" I asked.

"It's worse. At least they're working on cures for fatal diseases."

"What then?"

"He wants to become a fishing guide."

Sometimes in an interview, psychologists are required to put in extra effort to keep a straight face . . . uh, maintain our decorum.

I realized that, given my lust for angling and the risk admitting this might have on a potential client, my next question had to be purged of any interviewer bias or excess emotion and delivered in the most impartial, professional voice possible.

"Walleye or salmon?" I queried.

The woman gave me one of those long, penetrating stares clients reserve for the moment when they have confirmed their worst fear that shrinks need shrinks.

Realizing she'd seen through my professional facade, I acknowledged my prejudice toward fishing and offered to refer her to someone who played golf.

"Oh my God, no!" she cried. "My ex-husband played golf. But since you're a fisherman, maybe you can tell me why they're all so crazy."

I didn't take offense at the question. In a matter of a few minutes, I had explained that fishermen were no worse than most other sportsmen of passion, and they were considerably better off than many.

"How?" she asked.

"Well, they tend to be happier, more contented, and less stressed."

"They sound like milk cows," she mused. "But what about my son? He's obsessed with fishing and thinks of nothing else."

I smiled. "He may have a case of the passions."

"The 'passions'?"

"It's a kind of magnificent obsession with angling," I explained dreamily. "You see, fishing is always rewarding, always satisfying, always challenging, always . . ."

"Just a minute," interrupted the lady. "You sound as crazy as my son. And he gets that same stupid glint in his eye I see in yours. I tell you I'm worried. He's nineteen and should be in college. What do I do?"

Clients are always asking tough questions like this. For some reason, they want quick solutions to knotty problems. Fortunately, we psychologists are highly trained in dodging obvious queries. If you give advice and it works, you get the credit while the client becomes dependent and doesn't grow. If you give advice and it *doesn't* work, you come off looking stupid beyond belief. If things really go sour, you might get sued. Therefore, the answer to all requests for advice is to ask the same question you were just asked.

"What do you think you should do?" I asked.

"I don't know," said the woman. "Say . . . what *is* this? If I could get him to do what I want him to do I wouldn't be in here seeing you."

Another thing they teach in graduate school is how to handle frustrated and angry clients.

Once I explained to the woman I had always wanted to be a fishing guide myself, and that there was no way I could objectively consult her on how she might handle her son's request to spend his college savings on a twenty-foot jet boat, she accepted my referral to a non-fishing colleague and we terminated any professional relationship. Of course, I asked if she had one of her son's business cards, and I didn't charge her for the session.

Several years later, I ran into this woman in a department store. She'd lost the battle with her son, and he guided for a couple of years in Alaska before returning to the Lower Forty-Eight and starting college. Unless I miss my guess, he did not major in psychology.

RAISING FISHERMEN

Fishermen seem to spring up in non-fishing families with some regularity, as in the case I just described, but more often the child is aimed at the fishing life by its mother and father. Bull's-eyes are not guaranteed.

Though no one has ever asked me, I have always wanted to tell parents how to raise fishermen. As a father of three and consultant to many, I know about the vulnerabilities of little minds and, therefore, how to implant the sport of angling deep into the psychological core of an otherwise innocent child. As a one-time college instructor in developmental psychology, I am prepared to offer my own formula for rearing anglers. This formula also works to inoculate children against drug abuse and install self-esteem, subjects that will be further explained in a chapter on fishaholism.

NATURE VS. NURTURE

Are fishermen born to the sport or do they acquire the habit? Down through the centuries, people have pondered this and similar questions regarding great generals, opera singers, world-class athletes, and theoretical physicists.

Dr. John B. Watson, the famous behavioral psychologist and learning theorist, once said that if given enough time and total control of the environment, he could turn any given baby into a doctor, lawyer, or Indigenous chief.

Can you start with any old baby and turn it into a happy, contented, clear-eyed adult with a love of angling? Sure you can. The research says so. Down through the years Dr. Watson has been proved more right than wrong. Except for some hardcore personality traits and the limitations of genetically determined things like height and eye color, nurture wins.

There is no known anti-fishing gene. If anything, there is probably a pro-fishing gene, so raising fishermen should be no more difficult than raising Democrats. In the bargain, you can end up with an ethical sportsman who loves and respects nature and holds ecologically sound conservation values that last a lifetime.

What more, I ask any parent, could you possibly want?

START EARLY

You cannot begin your project too soon. Consider, for example, this fictionalized announcement from the *New York Times*:

"Born to Mr. and Mrs. Wendell P. Terry, an eight-pound, two-ounce fisherman. The baby angler was deftly netted by Dr. T. S. Morgan, himself a fly fisherman and longtime member of Trout Unlimited. The baby will be christened Lee Wulff Terry, after the world-famous fisherman of the same name."

There is great power in naming. In ancient times, names were so special they had to be given to you under extraordinary circumstances. Your name could come to you in a dream or be given you by an elder but, in any event, it was your name and only suited you. It set the course for your life.

Announcing the birth of a fisherman with a strong fishing name, in hopes of casting the die after nine months of pregnancy, though, is probably too late. To get a neonate headed in the right direction, you can actually begin well before the fetus is fully developed.

We know from several research studies that a little one is quite capable of learning while still in the oven. A fetus exposed to pieces by Beethoven while in the womb will, several years later, learn to play those same pieces more quickly than those who weren't, providing evidence human learning takes place in the womb. I used to tell my classes this old story about an English woman to drive this pre-birth learning point home.

There was once a newly pregnant woman who very much wanted her child to be both a fisherman and well mannered. To get the desired result, the lady read books on manners and stream etiquette to her swelling abdomen for the entire nine months of her pregnancy.

The nine months passed, but no child came. Then ten months. Then a year. Then two years and still no child. At the five-year mark, the lady was huge and quite uncomfortable, but there were still no signs of labor. A decade passed. Then two decades. After some thirty-five years, the lady passed away.

When the medical examiner opened her up, he found two fully grown English fishermen engaged in the following conversation:

"No, *you* go first."

"No, you. I insist. This is your beat."

"I'm very sorry, sir, but I believe it is your beat and, therefore, you should exit and take the first cast."

"Quite the contrary, my dear man. But thank you, anyway. Now, please, be a good sport, take your leave, and make the first cast."

This absolutely true story suggests several important steps that can be taken by couples hoping to raise an angler.

First, try to conceive the child during a fishing trip. I have no research to document the importance of environmental settings and their influence on matters of conception and eventual outcomes but how could it hurt?

Next, because positive in-utero influences have salutary effects, I cannot see the harm in the following prescriptions.

Expose the fisherman-in-progress to the sounds of water—babbling brooks, pounding surfs, waves lapping against canoe sides, etc.

Exposures to the sound of a screaming reel, shouts of "One on!" and the general sort of fishing chatter that accrues during a day on the water might give the tyke a leg up on angling jargon later on.

The mother-to-be should probably eat a lot of fish during the pregnancy.

Research has shown that both fetuses and infants are relaxed by the gentle swaying of the mother. What could better ready a child for a fishing future than easy hikes to remote lakes, the rocking motion of a boat, and the rhythmic action of Mom while she whips a fly rod back and forth, back and forth while whispering of rising trout, caddis hatches, and humming those joyful little tunes that sometimes bubble up from the heart during moments of great pleasure?

Both Mom and Dad might read fishing poems and stories to the swelling belly. As long as twins are not expected and you lay off the etiquette, what possible risks could there be?

GET THE BIRTH MYTH RIGHT

All of us have a birth myth. Sometimes the myth is given to us; sometimes we make up our own. For example, if three old guys in long beards are guided by a supernova to your mother's delivery room and happen to bring along some incense and myrrh, you're likely to grow up with a lot of people expecting you to do big things.

On the other hand, if you're in a quarrel with your parents about something and think they don't love you anymore, you may create your own birth myth. "There was a mix-up at the hospital. I'm someone else's kid." Or, "I must have been adopted."

A fisherman's birth myth might include being born on the opening day of walleye season, or at the height of the green drake hatch, or in the back of a bass boat. Being named "Izaak" after Izaak Walton or "Lee" after Lee Wulff also fit the bill.

Alexander the Great's birth myth was that he would conquer the world. This expectation was laid on him by his folks, some Macedonian soothsayers, and the fact of his royal birth, and after a little trouble in Asia Minor, he did conquer what he knew of the planet. Whether kings, conquerors, or casting champions, the process works the same. The important thing to remember is that parents have a great deal to do with what sort of myth the kid grows up with and, therefore, their destiny.

The birth myth the fisherman father hands to his offspring will typically include a number of psychological expectations, including the imagined warm companionship that will begin once the child is old enough to become "my little fishin' buddy."

This leads me to an observation about where the trouble begins for half of our population.

How many fathers look at a brand-spanking-new baby girl and think "fishin' buddy?" Not enough, I can tell you. More parents put a damper on things by seeing fishing as a "boy thing" or referring to angle worms as "icky." If you don't think of girls as fishers from the very start, the odds are heavily stacked against any little girl growing up to love the sport. Almost all the avid fisherwomen I know were brought to the sport by their fathers.

As we expect of children, so shall they grow.

If you want a daughter to grow up to fish with you, give her a fitting birth myth. If it's true, tell her she was born the day the first salmon returned to the river, the day the big pike was caught, or the morning the ice went out of the bay and the lake trout began to hit. Anything. Use visualization to set the goal.

If you're the trouter, close your eyes and "see" her standing side-by-side with you, knee-deep in your favorite stream. See a rod in her hand. See her dressed in hip boots, a light green vest, and wearing a yellow fishing hat with matching trim. See a smile on her bright little face. Now see that smile widen to a great grin as a nice rainbow rises to take her fly. To get what you want, follow Thoreau's advice: "Print your hopes upon your mind."

SETTING UP THE CLASSROOM

With a fishing birth myth in place, the next question is "How old should my child be before exposing them to angling?"

Very recent research on newborns indicates that, while we once thought they had poor and blurry vision in the first weeks of life, they actually see perfectly at a distance of nine inches. This is the approximate distance from the mother's breast to her face, and therefore the recommended distance for early exposure to fish pictures and fishing videos.

I'm speaking here of what psychologists call an "enriched environment." While a lot of research has been done on the possible beneficial effects of enriched stimulation, the results do not strongly support the idea that an especially busy, stimulating, enriched environment actually leads to things like a higher IQ. But then again, there's no data to suggest it hurts.

Early exposure certainly won't hurt. Of all the nursery rhymes my mother read me, this excerpt from one by Eugene Field most helped cast the die:

> *Wynken, Blynken, and Nod one night*
> *Sailed off in a wooden shoe;*
> *Sailed on a river of crystal light*
> *Into a sea of dew.*

"Where are you going, and what do you wish?"
the old moon asked of the three.
"We have come to fish for the herring fish
That live in this beautiful sea.
Nets of silver and gold have we."
Said Wynken, Blynken, and Nod.

The old moon laughed and sang a song
As they rocked in the wooden shoe,
And the wind that sped them all night long
Ruffled the waves of dew.

The little stars were the herring fish
That lived in that beautiful sea.
"Now cast your nets wherever you wish;
Never afeard are we!"
So cried the stars to the fishermen three:
Wynken, Blynken, and Nod.

· 19 ·

The Sense of a Woman

$\mathcal{M}$y father and his two brothers used to go salmon fishing together once a year out of Puget Sound. One year, they took my aunt Julia's brand-new Crown Vic to the docks. (Julia was out of town.) When they returned three days later, they were horrified to realize they'd left a bucket of bait in the trunk. In the summer. For three days.

Being guys (as well as a brew master, an insurance salesman, and a rear admiral), they knew immediately what to do. When they got home to Olympia, windows open all the way, they scavenged several bottles of perfume from Julia's dressing table, not realizing she was a connoisseur of fine fragrances. The combination of rotten minnows (or were they smelt?), Joy, Shalimar, Lui Guerlain, and Chanel No. 5 didn't work out as they'd intended. Uncle Carl parked the car on the street with a FOR SALE sign in the window and ordered a new Crown Vic from the Ford dealership in hopes it would arrive by the time Julia got home. No such luck, but that's a story for another day.

· 20 ·

The Fish Dog

My fish dog is a combination of Springer Spaniel and Hungarian sheepdog, as hairy a canine conglomeration as has ever gone afield. Being one-half bird dog and one-half work dog, he is good at neither hunting nor tending the flocks. Discovering this, I was content to let him remain curled up in a corner of the room where I couldn't tell his head from his tail. During that period, his only contributions to my fishing trips were a few locks from his long coat, which had a beautiful breathing action when tied into a streamer fly.

His name, Wolf, is derived from the fact that his face resembles a werewolf straight out of the Saturday night horror show, and not because he shares the characteristics of his canine cousins.

Occasionally, I would take Wolf along on a rabbit hunt. His uncontrollable enthusiasm actually worked to my advantage. If I could guess which way his next burst of speed would take him, I could position myself properly and let him drive the cottontails my way. It was a sort of rabbit-dog-hunter checker game.

I'll admit that I had wondered if his sheepdog ancestry might give him the desirable ability to herd brown trout. But remembering that trout have heels at which he could nip, I gave up on the idea.

Sheer accident was the way I discovered Wolf's affinity for trout. One warm spring morning I had arisen early and sipped a cup of coffee in the yard as I watched the sun perch on the horizon. "An ideal morning for a little fishing," I happened to think aloud.

Wolf broke into a howl, the likes of which were usually reserved for the Irish setter across the street. He obviously wanted to go along. But for what? His involvement in my fishing trips so far, not counting his hair for flies, had been in licking the tails of the trout I'd bring home. I relented. "Sure, Wolfer. You can go," I said, whereupon he sprung onto the hood of the car.

Creature of fishing habit that I am, I drove to a nearby stream that is my bent to flail. The river is a jungle of overgrowth and steep-sided banks. Occasional stretches of water are unencumbered with the thick overstory and allow room for a short backcast. It is in these areas that the brown trout will feed in the mornings and evenings. During the day they remain incarcerated in their jails of roots, branches, and undercuts.

I had turned Wolf loose in the nearby fields to chase butterflies and otherwise stay out of my way. I sat on the bank, looking for rises or other indications of trout activity. Should I encounter such omens, I fully intended to beguile the offending fish with a beautiful size-sixteen blue dun, which I would drop a foot or two above the trout's nose.

At last. As I watched a yellow warbler flit among the branches of a willow, it came. Slurp!

I swung my head in time to see the rings of disturbance riding the surface rapidly downstream.

Slurp!

This time on the other side of the hole.

Slurp! Slurp!

Instantaneously, I recalled the hundreds of facts that a fly fisherman must keep in his piscatorial computer when he moves into an ideal situation such as this. Fish the tail of the pool first. Wade softly. Cast smoothly. Don't spook the fish with the leader. Make sure the fly will float high.

The browns would be mine.

Directly behind me was an opening in the brush, obviously placed there by fate to allow my backcast. I stripped enough line from my reel so that my ten-foot leader would turn over properly. Everything was in tune, functioning perfectly. Measure the distance. The first cast counts. Now . . . this time.

I followed through with precision, and the fly dropped just short of a willow leaf and rode the water as would a natural insect that had fallen from the streamside vegetation.

I could see the brown trout on the river bottom. As the fly alighted, I thought I detected a nervous twitch in the fish's left pectoral fin. The fly floated on.

There. I was sure of it now. The brown flipped its tail and moved back a little to the left so as to be in better line of attack when the fly reached its position.

Slowly, the fish began to ascend, a look in its eye that I've seen in the orbs of truck drivers as they peruse the menu on the wall of the diner.

Cheeseburger—$1.95. Large French fries—90 cents. "Here it comes, brown trout," I thought. "Cheeseburger, fries, and a big malt. Put a rush on that order, Henry."

As the fish reached mid-depth, the speed of its ascent increased. Then, silhouetted against the azure May sky, an unidentified flying object appeared. True to a man intent on the matter at hand, I paid little attention. The depth perception out of the corner of my eye is not great, and the vision could have been a mosquito hovering near my hat brim or a Boeing 747 soaring at thirty thousand feet. Actually, it was a flying rag mop. It was Wolf.

His momentum must have been significant, because he sailed off the five-foot-high bank with the greatest of ease. His appearance coincided directly with the submergence of the trout. The brown was so close to taking the fly that, as it arched its back to descend, it scraped the point of the hook and left a small cycloid scale impaled there.

Sploosh!

Wolf has landed.

The temperature outside is sixty-one degrees and the time is 8:37 a.m. We hope you had a pleasant trip. Thank you for flying Wolf Air.

Wolf surfaced a few feet downstream from where he had entered. Helped by the current, the dog paddled my way. I remember thinking that if he were a spitz he should probably have been named Mark.

"Why are you just standing there?" every splash of his paws seemed to ask. "I flushed this big trout and I thought you would be catching it."

Using his floating ears as outriggers, he maneuvered onto shore. After mutual greetings, I noticed a bad sign.

The first symptom is a little twitch of the tip of Wolf's tail. By the time you see that, however, it is too late to take shelter. The quivers become convulsions as they travel toward his head.

The cold spray from Wolf's shower of river water sobered me that morning. And, although I didn't remonstrate with Wolf, I didn't have the craving to sneak up on any more fishing holes either.

I've taken Wolf on other fishing trips since then. But we have an understanding now. When he doesn't go, he knows that he'll have a fish tail or two to lick at day's end.

When he does go, I know that I'm fishing just for the fun of it.

Bowplunk Dogs

*O*ne of the more famous American ballast dogs is the bowplunk dog known as the Maine bow dog. This breed was originally recognized by Mr. Barnaby Porter of Damariscotta, Maine. With his kind permission, his breed standard is printed here for the first time, though I'm sure such a fine description has probably been printed in other places for the first time, too.

Observations on the Maine Bow Dog
by Barnaby Porter

It's time the Maine Coon cat was put in its place. It has been highly overrated as a breed all these years, and I'm not so sure anyone has a true and accurate idea of just what makes a coon cat a coon cat anyhow. It's an appellation that has come to have about as much meaning as "colonial farmhouse." Rather common-looking balls of fluff are what they are.

Of much more convincing pedigree is a hardy and noble breed of dog, heretofore not made much of because of its humble beginnings and conspicuous absence from the show ring. This is the magnificent Maine Bow Dog, his name deriving from his deeply ingrained habit of standing, proud and brave, on the bow of his master's boat as it plies the lively waters along the Maine coast.

There is nothing quite so moving as the sight of such a dog holding his station, ears flying and a big smile on his face, as his sturdy vessel bounds over the sparking whitecaps, his profile emblazoned on the horizon.

The points of conformation in the Bow Dog breed are far from strict. The dog's size, color and general appearance have nothing to do with it. Even pom-pom tails are allowed. Good claws are the only mandatory physical attribute. It's mostly a matter of character and carriage. The animal must have superb footing and balance, and most important, he must display the eagerness and bravery of the true Bow Dog. A passion for boats and the water is essential, for the dog must be willing and able to maintain the classic stance, chin up and chest out, in even gale force winds.

Individual Bow Dogs may vary greatly in style, but their dedication to duty must be unquestionable. One I know, named "Wontese," who looks something like a Springer Spaniel, is such a glutton for cold and punishing duty that his uncontrolled but enthusiastic chattering has become legendary. Another, named "Duke," wears a sou'wester. Remarkable, these dogs.

Being in the Working Dog class, Bow Dogs are permitted the occasional slipup to be expected in the real-world conditions under which they must perform. Mine, an almost flawless specimen, was most embarrassed

Bowplunk dog—before and after

one day when he broke stance for a brief moment to take a flea break. There was a blustery chop on the sea, and in a flash, he slipped ingloriously over the side, his gleaming claws raking the bow as he disappeared from sight. A valuable dog like that, I had to come around and fish him out of the waves. I hoisted his drenched bulk back aboard, and without so much as a thought about shaking off, he leaped up forward to where he belonged, brave and proud, ears flying.

That's a Maine Bow Dog if I've ever seen one. It made me proud to be his master.

Mr. Porter obviously knows his dogs, and he does a good job of reporting on the courage and nobility of this breed, which stands in the bows of fishing boats and looks good no matter what—even though there is great variability in the way they look. (This is lucky, however, because there is a similar variability in the looks of Maine fishing boats and even greater variability in the looks of Maine fishermen. Matching bow dog to boat should not be the problem it is with the Baildales.) Mr. Porter seems unaware that his dog belongs to a functional breed classically known as the ballast dog, and though he does realize that the breed is highly functional, he misses the connection between the dog's function and its "conspicuous absence from the show ring," since it is not registered with any kennel club in the world, so far as I know.

The purpose of a ballast dog standing in the bow (the front, or pointy end of the boat) is to hold it down in the water while you paddle or steer from the stern. (The reason it is called the "stern" is because it is a very serious part of the boat, being where you hang the outboard motor, and steer from.) Trolling (named after the character who fished under bridges when you were a kid) also takes place in the stern. Really good bow dogs have an innate sense of "trim." As the speed of the boat increases, the dog leans farther and farther forward, keeping the boat "trimmed," or relatively even in the water.

Mr. Porter was on the right track when he listed the problem areas in Maine bow dogs. He correctly points out that they should be agile, as well as able to concentrate for long periods of time and avoid fleeting distractions. This means a good Maine bow dog really ought not fall overboard. Natural selection would have taken care of this problem years ago, if only fishermen would just keep going and tend to business instead of forgiving a fallen dog. But the dog is half of a closely bonded team, and that attachment is rarely ruptured just because one member of the party made a mistake. Very few fishermen have the sheer Darwinian courage not to turn back in an attempt to rescue a fallen bow-wow, and this prevailing softheartedness has been a large factor in the dog's morphology: A successful bow dog has a hefty scruff.

22

Quotes from Famous People You Find in Other Fishing Books

Now you don't have to buy them. You're welcome.

> "Many men go fishing all their lives without knowing it is not fish they are after."
>
> —Henry David Thoreau

Can you imagine this quote included in the welcome to a bass fishing tournament?

> "Be patient and calm for no one can fish in anger."
>
> —Herbert Hoover

Bet old Herb never fished a party boat—not to mention, Dyson makes a better vacuum cleaner.

> "No life is so happy and so pleasant as the life of the well-governed angler."
>
> —Sir Isaac Newton

Did not just one but a bushel of apples fall on his head? This old angler even misspells "complete."

QUOTES FROM FUNNY PEOPLE YOU MIGHT FIND IN OTHER FISHING BOOKS BUT DESERVE REPEATING

"There is no use you walking five miles to fish when you can depend on being just as unsuccessful near home."

—Mark Twain

"Fishermen are born honest, but they get over it."

—Ed Zern

"There's a fine line between fishing and standing on the shore looking like an idiot."

—Stephen Wright

"What do you expect from a pastime where the very first thing you do is open a can of worms?"

—Henry Beard

"There is no greater fan of fly fishing than the worm."

—Patrick F. McManus

"Most of the world is covered by water. A fisherman's job is simple. Pick out the best spots."

—Charles Waterman

"Bass fishermen watch Monday-night football, drink beer, eat BBQ, drive pickup trucks, and prefer noisy women with big breasts. Trout fishermen watch *PBS NewsHour*, drink white wine, call vegetables veggies, drive little electric cars, and rarely think about women at all. This last characteristic may have something to do with the fact that trout fishermen spend most of the time up to their thighs in ice-cold water."

—Anonymous, who wishes to remain anonymous

Comatose, God of Fishing

*N*o sport has attracted the following among Scandinavian Americans that fishing has, and for good practical and theological reasons. First, all other sports require a lot of talking, running, or throwing things. Second, the state that other cultures and religions call "nirvana"—the condition of being at complete oneness with one's environment—is achieved by the Scandinavian only while fishing. Only fishing offers the perfect transcendental state: absolute silence (for lack of anything interesting to talk about), absolute motionlessness (rivaled only by rigor mortis), and a total intellectual and sensory deprivation (broken only by mosquitoes).

Ice Fishing

FISHING: RELAXING, OR COMA-INDUCING?

*F*ishing comes in three forms: ice, boat, and dock. All three rely on sensory deprivation for their entertainment value, except that you're generally coldest when you're ice fishing.

Ice fishing is the only form of abuse that does not get you into trouble with the law in Minnesota. This is because it is self-inflicted and because there are practical limits to the percentages of the population that can be put in jail.

There are two forms of ice fishing. Pure—or Unprotected—Ice Fishing involves only the individual fisherman, a hole in the ice that is constantly refreezing (a little hint from Mother Nature that fishermen seldom heed) and a piece of string.

Philosophers say that Pure Ice Fishing is a form of Scandi/Zen meditation where the pilgrim contemplates the oneness of the Universe and the numbness of their body parts.

Ethnologists say that the Unprotected Ice Fisherman is expressing a subconscious solidarity with the ethnic archetypes of his heritage. In English, this only means that he is freezing to death, just as his ancestor, Gorm the Very Cold, did in 734 near what later became Stavanger.

The other form of ice fishing—Protected Ice Fishing—gets its name from the huts the fishermen build to shelter themselves from both the cold and women. In fact, Protected Ice Fishing is really an excuse for grown men to play house. Not only do they play house, they play town.

When the local lake's ice reaches proper thickness, men hop into their pickups and drag their huts to a seasonally permanent location. Other men see these first huts, and soon the lake has so many huts that regular streets and avenues have formed, occasionally complete with street markers.

And there you have it: an instant town—but a town just as some men have fantasized it since their boyhoods—a self-regulating town with no bureaucrats and very few women.

These ice houses are decorated by men, for men. They feature no frilly craft items found in supermarket magazines, no cheery pastels, and no hanging things made of yarn. The ice-fishing house is the modern version of the Victorian hunting lodge. If ice houses today look more like the inside of a van than a grand lodge, you must bear in mind that neither the great wealth nor the fine Victorian sensibilities that built those old lodges are commonly to be found nowadays.

While ice-fishing houses do offer some improvement over sitting exposed to the elements on the ice pack, balancing the primal forces of frostbite against tribal starvation, it has been my experience that ice houses are still not all that comfortable.

While I understand that being a little uncomfortable is an important part of the celebration of maleness, I have always been tempted to celebrate my maleness in my perfectly warm house, with nice soft chairs, and just lie about how uncomfortable I was.

Instead of bundling up like a fool on a polar bear hunt, I could just ask my wife to go to a movie for a few hours because I wanted to be alone.

Then I could call some guys up and tell them to drive over in pickups so we'd all feel real macho. We'd just hang out at the house, have a few beers, pass the afternoon lying about how uncomfortable we were, and congratulate each other on how well we were taking it.

We'd stay warm, save the gas money to drive to the lake, and spare ourselves the terror of listening to the ice crack every time a pickup drove near our ice house.

I suppose there's a catch to this plan somewhere, but it sure makes sense to me.

· 25 ·

Jackrabbit Fishing

My big break in the field of outdoor writing came when I got the chance to interview Jim Dowden, the famed—nay, infamous—jackrabbit fisherman of Bozeman, Montana.

Anybody who has tried to break into the big three of the outdoor writing industry (in outdoor writers' jargon, that refers to *Outdoor Life*, *Sports Afield*, and *Field & Stream)* can tell you that they are tough nuts to crack. Even the editors of those magazines will tell you the same thing by way of a form-letter rejection slip. It is really simple arithmetic.

There are three magazines that buy, say, for the sake of discussion, one thousand articles each year. There are, say, for the sake of discussion, 4,186,745 outdoor writers. When you divide 1,000 by 4,186,745 you get . . . well, it is a very small number.

Editors tell new writers that if they come up with unusual stories, the kind that will make the busy reader pause long enough to buy the magazine, they may eventually see their words and their names in print.

That was my chance. My wife always told me I was unusual. First, I tried a manuscript about using pasta balls to catch carp imported from Italy. That went over like a can full of worms at a fly-fishermen's dinner.

Next, I sent a manuscript that dealt with the effect of the Solunar Tables on fishermen's wives. Apparently, based upon the number of rejection slips I acquired, that item was as popular as sand in a spinning reel.

I was as disillusioned as a guy who finds a misspelling in the dictionary.

Finally, I met Jim Dowden. I had been running article ideas through my brain long enough to recognize a winner when I stumbled on it. Dowden's career as a jackrabbit fisherman had not garnered a lot of press when I met him in a dimly lit roadhouse in Montana's Bitterroot Valley in the winter of '69. He was shooting nine-ball and quaffing a mixture of distilled liquids that would probably have burned in a camp lantern.

After beating me five straight games he looked up, just before he was ready to break, and said, "You ever fish for jackrabbits, bud?"

Well, of course, the answer was no. I was given and accepted a libated invitation to meet Dowden the next morning at a sagebrush flat crossroads where he would take me fishing for the huge bush bunnies.

When morning arrived, Dowden opened the trunk of his battered '55 Chevy and pulled out sections of a fly rod that, when put together, made up one of the longest and strongest whoosh-sticks I have ever seen. To the butt of the rod he attached what could be described more accurately as a winch than as a fly reel. On the reel was a length of reinforced fly line that ended in a wire leader.

Just one look at the assembled monstrosity and the viewer could easily see how Dowden had developed his massive upper body. A day of jackrabbit fishing with such a contraption was easily more of a workout than a day in the weight room at FATOFF, Inc.

I followed Dowden through the sagebrush. I was more intent upon watching and learning than in doing any actual jackrabbit fishing myself. I was content to put all my efforts into taking notes and snapping photographs of the encounter than in making the catch.

We hadn't been out for five minutes when Dowden stopped and cocked his left ear upwind. Something unheard by me had come to the attention of the crafty wielder of the desert fly rod.

"Listen," he said. "There's one feeding off to the left."

I listened but only to the silence of the desert, a silence that is sometimes so complete that it is deafening.

But Dowden was insistent. "Naw, he's up there," he remarked at my inability to hear the critter. "Sounds like he's working on some spring grass."

Dowden pulled a box from his jacket and began groping through the contents. I was certain from his actions that he knew what he sought, but it took him some time to find it.

"There it is," he shouted in a whisper, pulling a long, green, yarn-like wisp of a thing from what was obviously a fly box. "I haven't used this since I took a twelve-pounder down in the sage flats near Vernal."

Dowden reached for his tippet and deftly removed the orange carrot fly he had planned to use. On went the fake grass fly and he began to false cast.

There was a slight breeze blowing toward him, and it took the larruper of lagomorphs quite an effort to finally get enough line out. But then it was done and with a final thrust he used a double-haul and banged thirty-five yards of fly line through the Montana morning.

The green grass fly paused in the air and dropped to the sagebrush as softly as the closing of a baby's eyelids. There the fly hung. No action. Then Dowden pointed the rod tip directly at the fly and with smooth wrist action imparted a little side-to-side action to the grass fly. "Simulates the wind," he whispered from the side of his mouth, never taking his stare from the area of the fly.

Then, without so much as "getting a bite," Dowden pulled back on the rod. The reel began to sing as a full-grown white-tailed jackrabbit streaked through the sagebrush. Occasionally the rabbit's rear quarters would show as the critter bounded into momentary view. My motor-driven camera was clicking profusely.

To shorten what is becoming a long story, let me tell you that Dowden landed that rabbit as he had countless others, letting the bunny play itself out to the point of exhaustion.

It was a simple maneuver to remove the barbless hook from the jack's lip and shake the bunny a little until it revived and bounded on its merry way. Of course, Dowden occasionally keeps a rabbit for the pan, but in the last few years has leaned more and more to the catch and release theory.

"There's just not enough jacks in some areas to go around anymore," he said.

The day afield had been one of my most memorable. Although I wasn't able to score with the big three of outdoor magazines, the trip allowed me to be published in a new market, *Jackrabbit Fisherman's Annual*, a publication that has since gone out of business and put all of its back issues through the shredder.

26

BUMPER SCHTICKERS

A Day of Fishing Is Still Better than a Day of School/at Work/ with the In-Laws (Reader's Choice)

Old Fishermen Never Die, They Just Smell That Way.

It's Not How Deep You Fish, It's How You Move Your Worm!

I Spend My Day Off with an Ice Hole

Women Who Fish Make the Best Catch

I Caught the Big Fish You Lost

Education Is Important but Fishing Is Importanter

Good Things Come to Those Who Bait

Men & Fish Are Alike. They Both Get into Trouble When They Open Their Mouths.

Gut Fish?

Nothing Makes Me Happier Than Casting Over Your Line!

Reel Men Fish!

All Fishermen Are Liars Except You & Me and I'm Not Sure About You.

You Can Always Tell a Fisherman but You Can't Tell Him Much.

I Don't Always Tell People Where to Catch Fish but When I Do, I'm Lying.

What Do Alaskan Women Say about Alaska Fishermen? The Odds Are Good, but the Goods Are Odd.

Women Know Why Men Love to Go Fishing: It's the Only Time They Will Hear the Words "Wow, That's a Big One!"

More Chrome-Plated Wit

If You Give a Man a Fish, He'll Eat for a Day. If You Teach a Man to Fish, He'll Drink Beer All Day.

If You Give a Man a Beer, He'll Fish for an Hour. If You Give a Man a Half Rack of Beer, He'll Stay Out of the House for the Better Part of a Day.

Give a Man a Fish and You Feed Him for a Day. Don't Teach a Man to Fish and Feed Yourself. He's a Grown Man. Fishing Is Not That Hard.

If You Give a Man a Fish, He'll Eat for a Day. If You Teach a Man to Fish, He'll Still Eat All the Fish You Caught for Yourself.

Give a Man a Fish and He'll Eat for a Day. Teach a Man to Fish and He'll Eat for a Lifetime. Give a Man a Religion and He Will Die Praying for a Fish.

If You Teach a Man to Fish, He'll Fish for a Day. If You Teach a Man to Fly-Fish, He'll Turn into a Woman. (Last Seen in a Parking Lot of a Bass Tournament.)

Teach a Man to Fish, He'll Finally Learn Something.

Give a Man a Fish and He'll Forget the Lesson.

Rainbow Trout Obituary

SMOKE HOLE, W. VA—three-pound rainbow trout, age three, of Low-Water Bridge Hole, succumbed Saturday after mistaking a metal spinner for real food.

Born in January of 1994 at the Reed Creek Hatchery in Pendleton County, Mrs. Rainbow was the daughter of the late Mr. and Mrs. Brood Trout. Surviving are thousands of siblings in such waters as Lost River, Thorn Creek, Seneca Creek, and the North Fork of the South Branch of the Potomac.

Mrs. Rainbow was best known for her ability to capture and ingest sculpin from between rocks at the bottom of the river.

A memorial photograph of Mrs. Rainbow will be placed on the wall of the angler who caught her. The State of West Virginia will honor Mrs. Rainbow with a Trophy Fish Citation including artwork by Duane Raver.

Full Circle

*A*n ebullient Texan went to Alaska to catch some braggin'-size fish. Way past his expectations he caught a seventy-five-pound king salmon. At the bar that night, he was telling about his whopper and the barkeep replied: "Well, fella, everything in Alaska is bigger than Texas. If we divided Alaska in half, then Texas would be the third largest state."

"Yeah, yeah," retorted the Texan, "so I been hearing. How about a small beer?"

The bartender brought him a glass of beer, which held at least a quart.

"I asked for a small beer," snorted the Texan.

"That *is* a small beer in Alaska," replied the bartender. "Remember, everything is bigger in Alaska."

Later, the Texan ordered a small steak. One came that filled a large platter. "I know," said the Texan, "everything is bigger in Alaska."

Later, full of beer, he asked where the men's room was. "Second door down the hall," he was told. Woozy, he went in the third door, staggered into a big, dark room, and fell into a swimming pool. He could be plainly heard, shouting at the top of his voice: "DOOON'T FLUSH IT!"

A fisherman had been chunking big plugs for muskies all morning without so much as a follow. Disgusted, he decided to halt for lunch and pulled over under the shade of a mammoth sycamore tree.

As he munched a sandwich, he happened to glance at the root of the big tree and was puzzled to see a hickory nut right at the water's edge. As he pondered, "What was a hickory nut doing beneath a sycamore tree?" he saw a squirrel scramble down the tree and crawl up to the nut. At that moment, a huge muskie shot from the water, seized the squirrel in its toothy jaws, and disappeared from sight. He hardly believed what he had just seen and wished he could have filmed it. Again, he wondered how that nut got there. Then he saw a big swirl close by the same root. Out of the swirl emerged the big, toothy head of the muskie, and it gently put the hickory nut back on the root.

You and I laugh. Muskie fisherman says, "What is so funny about that logical experience?"

The only weekend this rabid angler didn't go fishing was the one when he got married and went on his honeymoon. They were headed for his remote fishing cabin in the hill country when it started to rain in torrents. There was a stretch of road that was dirt, and it became so slippery their tires had no traction. So the groom said: "Honey, we've got to use our clothes to put down to make our tires hold, or we'll be stranded here all night. Let's start with your bridal gown."

Reluctantly she took off the gown. He put it under the rear wheels and they gained a few feet. Next, he used her slip, bra, and panties to gain a couple more yards. Then came his five-hundred-dollar country-western outfit, his underwear, plus his ten-gallon hat, to gain several more feet. They were just a few feet from the pavement and the only item left was his lizard cowboy boots. "Honey," he said, "Tell you what . . . these boots cost a thousand bucks, and I just can't part with them. But I've got an idea. See that light up there? Someone's home in that little cabin. Take these boots with you and see if you can make a deal for them to tow us out of this mess."

In her birthday suit, she made her way through rain to the cabin door. She knocked and before an old-timer opened the door, she covered her nudity by placing the uppers of the cowboy boots between her legs, with just the soles and heels showing. Grasping the boot bottoms between her hands, she looked up at the old-timer, smiling.

He cocked his head and said: "Something wrong, ma'am?"

She came back: "Yes, you see, we're on our honeymoon and my husband got stuck!"

The old-timer looked her over with a quizzical eye and queried: "Well, ma'am, have you tried holding your nose and blowing?"

Catfish fishermen have to be the raunchiest-smelling of all because they use the stinkiest baits. Like leaving shrimp or liver to age on the back porch until the neighbors complain and the buzzards are circling outside.

This particular catfisherman arrived home with a baby skunk under his arm. "Marthy," he said to his wife, "this here little skunk was wanderin' along the road and I knew it would die without its mama, so I brought it home. Do you suppose you could find a way to feed it tonight?"

His wife smiled and replied: "Why yes, I could use our daughter's little doll bottle, should be about the right size." She warmed some milk and the little bottle worked beautifully. But she thought . . . I wonder if it's against the law to keep a baby skunk? So she phoned the game warden and asked him.

He replied, "No, ma'am, that's a very nice thing you're doing, otherwise that little skunk probably would die. But it does raise a question. How will you keep it warm tonight without its mama?"

She said, "Well, I'll just put it in bed between me and Pa. That ought to keep it warm."

The game warden shot back, "But, ma'am, what about the smell?"

And she replied: "Well, heck, let that little skunk get used to it . . . the same as I had to!"

30

Crazy Fishing

*M*ost fishing trips are pretty ordinary. We catch something or we don't, and either way, we return home largely content, having nourished our obsession yet another day. When Izaak Walton wrote *The Compleat Angler* 345 years ago, he recognized that there was far more to fishing than fish, and he called his favorite pursuit a contemplative recreation. Alas, his discourse does not divulge whether his angling ever gave him more to contemplate than he anticipated—or appreciated. Certainly mine has.

There was that time, for example, when one of my casts wound up in the creek behind a pond's dam, having traveled all the way through the drainpipe. Now that was something to contemplate. Some of my catches have also been a bit unusual. Then, too, there was that business that took place in a roadside ditch, when . . . well, I'll get to that later.

The drainpipe incident took place years ago, on an unseasonably warm winter afternoon. Given the time of year, I had no great expectations, but I thought I might be able to dredge up a bass or two in a nearby pond by fishing a weighted plastic worm in the deep water along the dam. Besides, it was a pleasant day to be out. After going nearly an hour without a strike, however, I sat down opposite the drainpipe and began casting methodically, reeling very slowly. One other fisherman showed up, but he wasn't catching anything either.

I was daydreaming when I felt the unmistakable thump that signals a strike. I immediately opened the bail on my spinning reel to let the bass take the worm before setting the hook. Line poured off the spool. Boy, that was one fast-moving fish. When it showed no signs of slowing down, I closed the bail and set the hook. Nothing. Must have dropped the worm, I thought. I didn't think the bass had felt the hook, so I opened the bail again just in case. Line streamed out of the guides, faster than ever. By this time, the other fisherman had walked over to watch. I set the hook a second time, but there was no resistance.

"How come your line is going into that drainpipe?" he asked.

"It can't be in the pipe," I answered. "I didn't even cast in that direction."

"Looks like it to me," he said. I looked closely, and it certainly appeared that my line went directly to the top of the pipe, which was level with the water's surface. I began to reel, and after what seemed an eternity, the worm popped out of the pipe. The fisherman eyed me for a moment, then gathered up his gear and left.

I sat for several minutes trying to figure out how such a thing could have happened. Finally, I made another cast and watched in amazement as the mystery unraveled. A light breeze slowly blew the floating coils of loose line toward the mouth of the pipe. The line drifted across the top of the pipe and lodged against a bit of trash. I began to reel and shortly saw my worm climb over the lip and plop in. That plop had been my strike. I opened the bail, and somewhere deep in the bowels of the dam, my plastic worm yanked yards of line off the reel as it raced down the pipe and into the creek behind the dam. I went home, where I eyed myself suspiciously in the bathroom mirror.

Looking back, I can see a similar logic at work behind all the strange events that have happened to me while I was fishing—there's never been any inscrutable cosmic mystery, just relentless coincidence. Consider that summer day some years ago when I was surf fishing. The fishing wasn't very good, and after reeling in to check my bait—it was untouched—I set the rod in the sand spike and walked up the beach a short distance to stretch my legs. I didn't at first connect the woman's scream with the tight arc in my spinning rod. I thought a fish had grabbed my bait in the backwash of suds, and besides, the woman was fifty yards down the beach chasing a poodle.

I ran to the rod and grabbed it, at which point I noticed that my line ran straight to the dog. I had never, until that moment, considered that a poodle would eat a raw shrimp, especially one with a hook in it. My instinctive reaction to set the hook wasn't without benefit since the dog, slowed by the drag, proved easier for the woman to catch on its second run (for what it's worth, poodles don't fight much, and this one didn't jump even once). There was nothing to do then but give them both lots of slack line and await the consequences. Fortunately, when the lady arrived with my catch, I was able to get the hook out without using pliers. While I listened attentively as she made some suggestions to me, her poodle ate the rest of my shrimp. Hearing of the incident later, one friend commented that this was a prime example of why fishermen should always carry a gaff.

Another interesting catch was far less traumatic, but it fits the pattern. Almost no one used a fly rod in salt water thirty years ago when I walked out one summer day on the Fort Macon jetty to try my new nine-foot, ten-weight rod equipped with a three-hundred-grain, high-density shooting head. Friendly fishermen gave me room to cast, curious to see whether I would catch anything, especially since no one seemed to be having much luck soaking bait or casting lures. I doubt they'd ever seen anyone use a fly rod in salt water. After about a dozen casts, I had a solid strike on a Lefty's Deceiver streamer fly that I had been working slowly along the bottom.

"Got one," I said, in case someone might not have noticed. The fight was strong, though sluggish, but whatever I had hooked ran off to one side a short way, then reversed direction. It did this several times, giving me cause to suspect that it was most likely a flounder or spotted sea trout. You can imagine my surprise when I slid a size ten-and-a-half low-heeled canvas tennis shoe onto the rocks. It was hooked in the tongue, which was not only appropriate but also provided the fulcrum that had caused the shoe to plane first one way and then the other. It had been a convincing performance, and we all looked at the shoe for several stunned moments until finally one of the other fishermen found the right words.

"You oughta cast back out there," he said. "Them kind normally run in pairs."

Fishermen have been catching footwear—mostly old boots—long enough for it to become a cartoon cliché, but bagging the wahoo of the genus struck everyone as being nearly unique. The same, as I was soon to discover, might be said for appliances.

Not long after I caught the tennis shoe, I was fishing for flounder on the Emerald Isle Pier with some of the regulars I had come to know over the years. We each tended several rods baited with live jumping mullet in the slough just off the beach, and occasionally we would check a rod by reeling up the slack to see if we still had bait or if we could feel any resistance that might indicate that a flounder had eaten the minnow. As I was doing this, I felt the line tighten. I set the hook.

"Got one," I said (this is an egocentric habit that clearly needs to be broken). The rod bent sharply, and everyone rushed to the rail to see what I had hooked. It was soon obvious that this was no flounder because we could see a wide, silvery flash now and then as the fish darted back and forth several feet down in the green water.

"Looks like a bluefish, or more likely a big pompano or jack," someone said. The drop net was lowered, and everyone waited while I struggled to gain line. Moments later, the chrome-plated top of a drinking fountain cleared the water and was dutifully netted and slowly hoisted over the rail. It hit the pier with a resounding clang. The hook was caught in the drain hole in the center of the fountain top, causing it to slip-slide back and forth. I don't recall precisely what was said about this catch, though there may have been some mention of a rare hybrid between a horseshoe crab and a squid that propels itself by squirting water.

I have had other experiences that, while they don't defy explanation, are clearly cause for contemplation. Mike Caddis and I were bass fishing one day when we pulled up to a likely looking stump. I cast to one side of the stump, and he cast to the other. He caught an eight-pound bass.

"I know why you didn't catch this fish," he said as he admired his catch, then turned it around for me to see. "Look here."

The eye socket—the eye that would have been able to see my lure—was empty.

As for the incident involving the roadside ditch, it occurred back in the 1970s when my friend Melvin Kennedy first began fly fishing for mountain trout. Though I was not much more than a novice myself, I offered to go with him and share what little I had learned.

"Trout aren't really hard to catch if you know how to read the water and determine which spots they like," I remember telling him, no doubt quoting some famous angling author. After reading the water over a two-mile stretch of river, Mel still hadn't caught a trout. And though he hadn't actually seen me catch one, he graciously allowed that he was certain I had. Discouraged, we left the stream and began walking back down the road to the camp.

"I think you must have a secret fly you're not telling me about," Mel said.

"No, really, I don't," I replied. "I haven't caught any—I mean, many—and there's certainly nothing magic about this fly. You just need to get the knack of letting your fly float naturally without dragging on the surface. A dragging fly spooks trout."

To illustrate my point, I stepped over to where a tiny spring run passed through a culvert under the road. The trickle was barely six inches wide and no more than an inch or two deep, except for a bucket-sized pothole under the end of the protruding culvert. With only a few feet of leader hanging from the rod tip, I lowered the fly onto the glassy boil.

"See, you need to let it float freely like this so that—"

Slam! A five-inch wild brook trout grabbed the fly and dangled quivering in front of us.

"Honest, Mel, I never . . ." I stammered.

Mel looked first at the trout, then at me. Finally, he said what any fisherman would have said: "You're going to try to sell me that fly, aren't you?"

31

515 Miles and No Trout

(Let's Be Frank)

NIGHTMARES IN WYOMING

You don't have to travel halfway around the world to get confused by fly fishing. I can honestly say—and excuse me if this sounds like bragging—that I've been puzzled and bewildered by fly fishing in Alaska, Colorado, Montana, Wyoming, and the Dakotas—North Dakota, South Dakota, East Dakota, and even West Dakota.

I think it's because I have not become really scientific about the sport; like, say, Frank Plucinsky of Pennsylvania, who is featured in an ad in the February 2001 issue of *Fly Fisherman* magazine. In this ad there's a big photo of Frank. Under his chin are these words: "My diary has a record of every hatch I've fished for twenty-six years." This makes him different from me in the sense that under my chin are more chins.

The ad, for Sage fly rods, goes on to say: "If it flies, flits, or flutters, trout fisherman Frank Plucinsky knows it by name (in both Latin and English, of course). In fact, he knows life on Pennsylvania's Tulpehocken Creek so well that he can tell you when the caddis are on just by the blooming of Virginia bluebells that grow along its banks."

I do not even know what Virginia bluebells are. Although my cousin Tony, who lives in Roanoke, told me he once had a really bad case of Virginia blue *ba!*—uh, let's just say he was single and lonely.

The point is, Frank has written down detailed descriptions of every insect hatch he has encountered in the past twenty-six years of fly fishing. I, by way of comparison, cannot remember where I was last night or, at this moment, my middle name. So I cannot compete with fly fishermen such as Frank. (Which is why avid fly fishermen sometimes refer to dynamite and a heavy stick as "the great equalizers.")

I'm just kidding, of course. I am a big proponent of catch-and-release. Well, you know, I would be if I could ever *catch*.

Take a recent fly-fishing adventure. I took with my equally inept fly-fishing friend Mike Anton. Like most Americans, we caught no trout during that particular six-day period in May. What made us different, perhaps, is that we drove 515 miles, during that time period, along some of the greatest trout streams in Colorado and Wyoming, often stopping, getting out, putting on our waders and vests, and trying to catch trout. We fished up to ten hours each day, stopping only occasionally to down a quick meal of Prairie Dog McNuggets. (Did I mention we spent part of the trip in Wyoming?)

Anyway, here now, just like Frank Plucinsky's diary, is a summary of that particular trip.

Wednesday, May 10

> 2 p.m.: Stand near window in newsroom of newspaper where I work in Colorado and shout, "Look, it's Jimmy Hoffa!" When everyone runs to window, I sneak out back door, meet Mike, and leave on fishing trip. As we drive away, boss Cliff has sent team of reporters to ask the twenty-five-year-old sandwich truck driver across the street if he is Jimmy Hoffa.
>
> 6:30 p.m.: Arrive in Laramie, Wyoming.
>
> 7:00 p.m.: Check out Laramie cultural district.
>
> 7:08 p.m.: Depart Museum of Rodents.
>
> 7:30 p.m.: Stroll into Buckhorn Saloon, look at patrons, become frightened.
>
> 7:45 p.m.–9 p.m.: Mingle nervously with locals. Gain valuable insight into technique for field dressing an elk using only your teeth and a bottle opener.
>
> 9:30 p.m.: Find cheap motel, go to sleep.
>
> 10 p.m.–7 a.m.: Have nightmares about Wyoming. In worst one, I am a sheep.

Thursday, May 11

Arrive in remote Saratoga, Wyoming. Sign reads POPULATION 1969, which is, as it turns out, also the fashion year residents are stuck in.

> 11 a.m.: Wade confidently into famed North Platte River.
>
> 1:15 a.m.: Return to truck. Wring out pants and shorts. Put on waders.
>
> 11:30 a.m.–3 p.m.: Serious fishing in "Blue Ribbon" river. Catch nothing. Blame this on wind, inability to match the hatch, and unbelievably finicky trout. Local anglers we encounter believe repeatedly slipping on moss-covered rocks and falling into the river may also have played small role.

Friday, May 12

> 6 a.m.: Determine North Platte River has no trout. See sights on nearby Saratoga Lake. Local fly-shop owner says lake contains lots of five-pound rainbows and browns. We ask how cold the lake water is and whether a man could "freeze to death if he repeatedly fell into it." He asks why that would concern us. We tell him to mind his own business.
>
> 6 p.m.: No trout in Saratoga Lake, either. Return to car. Wring out hats. See more local anglers, clutching their midsections, pointing at us, and laughing in what appears to be some sort of "Wyoming welcome."

Saturday, May 13

> 6 a.m.: Return for another shot at Saratoga Lake. I am swayed by fishing partner's argument that it seemed "easier to swim back to shore in the lake than in the fast-moving river."
>
> 10 a.m.: Return to car. No trout. Crowd of local well-wishers now estimated at three hundred. They send up wild roar as we wring out our hats. We climb into truck and hit the road, vowing to return "when the fishing improves."
>
> NOON: Leave Wyoming, cross into Colorado. Sign reads: WELCOME TO COLORADO. PLEASE WIPE YOUR FEET BEFORE ENTERING.

2 p.m.: Arrive at famous Blue River. Desperate to do better, we take out insect screens, turn over rocks, and carefully examine the aquatic creatures we find.

4 p.m.: Sure beyond any reasonable doubt exactly which insects trout are not feeding on.

6 p.m.: Arrive at South Plate River near town of Hartsel, which combines Native American words *har* ("Who") and *tsel* ("took all the trees?"). In South Platte River, actually see huge trout rising to insect hatch that I'm sure Frank Plucinsky has made forty pages of notes about.

7 p.m.: No trout.

Hate Frank Plucinsky.

• 32 •

"Uh-Oh!"

(And Other Things Guides Shouldn't Say)

*D*uring lunch on a guided float trip recently, several of us client-anglers got into a contest that consisted of thinking up the worst things we might hear from guides. Following is a sample of guide remarks with a tendency to cause concern for clients.

The most common guide utterance, we agreed, was "Uh-oh!" To which the clients yell, "What? What!" The guide then replies, "Nothing." Knowing he has to be lying, you are consumed by worry for the rest of the trip. If you are fortunate, you never learn of the calamity you managed to escape.

One of my own experiences with a guide's "Uh-oh!" occurred on a drift-boat trip down a river in quest of steelhead. As we approached the takeout, our guide looked up and saw a small band of game wardens checking catches and licenses. "Uh-oh!" he said.

"What? What!" we hissed at him.

"Nothing," he said. "But listen, guys, let's just pretend that I'm not actually guiding you, okay? We're just a bunch of friends out fishing together, okay?"

It should have been fairly easy to pretend that our guide wasn't a guide, because we hadn't had so much as a nibble all day. Despite my reputation, however, I become extremely upset at even the hint of illegality or irregularity. I am also a very poor actor, particularly when it might come to covering up said illegality. Not knowing what our guide's possible crime might consist of—certainly not catching more than our limit of steelhead—I assumed it must be something to do with his guiding license. Either he had allowed it to lapse or he never had one in the first place. As it happened, I knew several of the game wardens at the takeout and during the backslapping and joyous cries at our surprise meeting, I glanced around for our "guide." Both he and his boat had vanished downstream toward the Pacific Ocean. I have not laid eyes on him since. Perhaps he drifted out to sea and rowed to Mexico.

Speaking of Mexico, I have had many superb guides there and caught many fish as a result of their excellent service. One time I took two of my daughters, ages twelve and sixteen at the time, on a guided fishing trip out from the little town of Barra de Navidad. (It was little back then.) Our guide was ancient and the boat maybe twice as ancient. At one point, the motor stopped and the old man began tinkering with it. Then he looked up at the rocks toward which we were drifting. I looked at the same rocks. Waves were crashing against them in an impressive manner. Then the old man uttered the Spanish equivalent of "Uh-oh!"

"What's he saying?" one of my daughters asked.

"Nothing," I said.

Then the guide spoke again, his eyes pleading with me. I managed to pick up the word *destornillador,* a word not that easy to pick up. I think he was asking if I happened to have a screwdriver on me. I didn't, which was odd, since I almost always carry a screwdriver.

I shook my head no in Spanish.

Fortunately, the old man managed to get the motor going while we were still a good nine inches away from the rocks. Despite that close call, our guide turned out to be a fishing genius as well as a great mechanic, even without a *destornillador.* Among our other nice catches that day was a large needlefish. You have to be a true fisherman to think of a needlefish as a nice catch. I used a portion of it as bait while casting off a beach that night. The needlefish was snapped up by a huge *pargo,* the Mexican equivalent, I believe, of a red snapper. I traded the fish to Rosario, the owner of a beachfront restaurant, for all the garlic-shrimp dinners we could eat. It was all very wonderful. Still, my memory of that little fishing excursion remains dominated by the guide's utterance of "Uh-oh!" It is a guide expression neither easily ignored nor easily forgotten.

Sven and Ole

Ole and Lena were out ice fishing one day, and Ole ran out of snoose so he asked Lena if she'd go across the lake and get some more from Sven's General Store. After she left, Ole called Sven on his cell phone and explained that Lena was coming his way, but she would have to charge it as he didn't send any money with her. When Sven heard that he asked why not; Ole explained, "I didn't know how thick the ice was!"

Ole died, so Lena went to the local paper to put a notice in the obituary section. The fellow at the counter offered his condolences and asked what she wanted to say about Old Ole. She replied, "Just put in 'Ole dead.'"

The newspaper man was puzzled. "That's it? Just 'Ole dead'? Surely, as long as you two were together, you'd want to say something more about Ole. The first five words are free!"

Lena thought for a few minutes and said, "Okay, put in 'Ole dead. Boat for sale.'"

The Fish Aren't Biting Very Hard

Ole and Sven are fishing at a secret lake that has lots of hungry fish in it. The only problem is the lake is surrounded by trees and brush, so it's hard to cast without getting snagged.

"I took the back treble hook off my Rapala minnow lure," Ole says. "Now I don't get snagged in the trees as much."

Sven nods. "I'm getting snagged even less."

Ole has caught three fish in the half hour they've been fishing. Sven has had some bites but hasn't caught anything.

After another thirty minutes, Ole has caught two more fish, but Sven still hasn't caught any.

"Would you like to try one of my lures?" Ole offers.

"No, I'll keep using this one. I keep getting strikes but the fish keep getting off. It's like they're not biting very hard today," Sven says.

A minute later, Sven suddenly has a big pike on the line. It pulls hard and jumps, then spits out the lure.

As Sven reels in his line, Ole sees his lure. "Sven, it doesn't look like you have any hooks on your lure. Did that pike bite them off?"

"Nope. You took a hook off to get snagged less. I made mine even more snag-proof. I took off both hooks."

Fish Don't Know Time Zones

Ole and Sven are having good luck fishing out on the Missouri River in South Dakota. They're catching walleyes—big big ones—which is like Minnesota Valhalla even though they're in South Dakota.

As it's getting dark, Ole observes that if they fished on the western side of the river the next evening, they could gain an hour of fishing time because of the time-zone change.

"Sounds good to me," Sven says. "Let's do that!"

The next night, an hour before dark, they land the boat on the river's east side, in the central time zone, drive across a bridge to the western side, in the mountain time zone, and relaunch the boat. They just get fishing and it gets dark.

"Gee, that hour went by fast," Sven says.

"Time flies when you're having fun?" Ole replies.

"So which side do we fish on tomorrow?" Sven asks as they head to shore.

"We start over here on the west side, of course," Ole says. "It gets light an hour earlier."

Sven nods.

"Unless you want to sleep an hour longer?" Ole adds. "Then we should start in the central time zone on the east side?"

"Good thing fish don't know time zones," Sven replies. "We're fooling them and fishing longer."

"Yeah, the fish don't have a clue what we're doing," Ole says smartly.

"Say, if we wanted to fish even later tomorrow night," Sven says, "we could set our watches for eastern time."

"Good idea. But why stop there? How about we set our watches for Iceland time?"

"Oh, now there's a brilliant idea?" Sven replies. "We'll be able to fish past midnight."

- Wet Fly Fishing -

· 36 ·

Bullheads

Although it is known as the land of 10,000 lakes, Minnesota has more poets than it does lakes and more gophers than it does poets. There are more Northerns than walleyes in the lakes. There are more bullheads than the total of Northerns, walleyes, gophers, and poets. Bullheads appear to be outnumbered by carp, but carp have an obsession with being seen. Walleyes make better eating than Northerns, but bullheads are easier to catch. Carp are the easiest to catch, because they swim on the surface and have a romantic notion about mortality. It is illegal to throw a carp back in the water. Most people throw them on the shore. If you step on a rotten carp, you never forget it.

Bullheads are called Iowa walleyes because Iowans have been known to spend their whole vacations camped at a Minnesota bullhead lake. There's no limit on bullheads. But more poems are published in Minnesota every year than bullheads are eaten by Iowans. There's no limit on Minnesota poets, but not even Iowans have a taste for them. More poems are eaten by Minnesotans than are read by them.

The best way to catch bullheads is to pack a bag of baloney sandwiches and potato chips, fill a beer cooler, apply mosquito repellant, and cast from a lawn chair on the shore. Trolling with a daredevil would be foolish and you might snag a Northern. Throw your line out with a light sinker and drag it slowly. When you feel a tug, set the hook. Bullheads don't strike and they don't fight. Poets fight more than bullheads, but they rarely strike. If you get one on the line, they stay there. If the bottom is weedy, use a bobber.

The best bait for bullheads is a night crawler. The best bait for poets is a promise you will sit and listen to them read from their new manuscript. Bullheads don't write poems, or at least they have enough sense to hide them in a drawer with their underwear. We would know by now if carp wrote poetry, because their concept of romantic mortality would drive them to publish it.

37

Where Are You, Ralph?

$\mathcal{T}$he second thing you notice is that no one is talking anymore. The predawn joviality at the dock begins to peter out just about the time you pass the sea buoy. A solemn, almost ominous stillness settles on the anglers as they become entranced by the foamy wake and the rhythmic roar of the diesels. One would think this is a particularly reflective group of fishermen, quietly appreciating the raw power of the open sea. It is a bit less than that.

This unlikely moment of dignity is the result of the first thing you noticed as the boat began to pick up the roll of the sea—that that there was a funny little acrid taste in the back of your mouth somewhere along the base of the tongue, and your throat seemed to be ever-so-slightly swollen. Well, you thought, the joke I was about to tell will keep. Just getting my sea legs, you know. I'll be fine. Is Portugal really out there? How fascinating.

I know this brand of hearty optimism very well. You can set your watch by what will happen to me next. Within three minutes, I will have bolted for the lee gunnel and be tossing groceries to the four winds. And isn't it precious beyond all words how those who are seldom afflicted describe the experience? We are said to be "barfing," "hurling," "calling Ralph," "tossing our cookies," "blowing lunch," and, my favorite, "chumming."

I envy those who never get seasick. My ruling passions are old ships, the wine-dark sea, and fishing, and yet I invariably get sick half a mile off the beach. Some sea captain I would make—Patrick O'Brien's hero Jack Aubry would cut me adrift if I sullied one of the holystoned decks of his frigate, the HMS *Surprise*. Since I was ten years old, I have built wooden model sailing ships, but if I so much as hold a twenty-inch brig in front me and give it a bit of a rocking motion, I get cross-eyed.

No problem, you say. Just take a seasickness remedy. Try Dramamine, Dramamine II, Marezine, or one of the newer prescription patches you stick behind your ear. Fine, except the only ones that work for me also put me to sleep. I once took Dramamine an hour or so before we were to go offshore. Because of heavy seas, the captain called off our trip at the last minute, so we went to the inlet to fish. I passed out for hours on the hot sand in 95-degree heat. The circling buzzards woke me at dusk.

On a trip this past summer, I thought I had found the answer in some of these newer remedies that are not supposed to make you sleepy. Indeed, we'd gotten almost all the way to the Gulf Stream and I was feeling wide-awake and cocky until I realized that I needed to tie an Albright special before I would be ready to fish for dolphin with flies. By the time I'd finished tying that knot, I knew I would shortly have an opportunity to enjoy my breakfast yet again.

Of course, most people can do some things to forestall or lessen the effects of seasickness, although they haven't worked all that well for me. First, by all means take medication in advance. Your pharmacist or doctor can make recommendations, and you'll need a prescription for the patches anyway. Seasickness remedies work very well for most people, but I would try to avoid those that warn of drowsiness—why pay six hundred dollars for an offshore nap?

A few other tips may help. Stay in the open air, chew gum, and watch the horizon if you feel queasy. Don't go below, where the stench of toilet chemicals will surely do you in. Also, avoid standing just above the diesel exhaust. There are two schools of thought on eating: Some say eat a light breakfast, while others suggest hearty fare on the theory that it at least gives you some ammunition. I'm not prepared to make specific recommendations, but perhaps you will recall what the ever-thoughtful Tweety Bird offered Sylvester when the latter was in the early throes of mal de mer. "Here, Puddy," said Tweety. "You look like you could use a nice piece of greasy pork."

The one bout of seasickness I remember above all others took place out of Morehead City more than thirty years ago on an old converted PT boat named the *Dance*. I had worked that summer to save money for a head boat trip, and sick or not, I was determined to fish. Indeed, I was doing fairly well until I mistook my box lunch for some ripe squid (the sandwiches and bait were passed out in identical paper cartons). I barely made it to the rail, where I managed to throw up right into the gaping maw of a very nice red snapper that another fisherman had just winched to the surface.

The angler was livid and refused to bring the fish aboard. Instead, he cut his line and stalked off to try his luck from another spot along the rail.

I was too sick to enjoy this at the time, but I recall thinking that he could have rinsed off that snapper. Besides, I would have swapped him a brace of untainted black sea bass for it. After all, it isn't often you catch the main course and the stuffing at the same time.

38

Tying It All Together

If you become an avid fly angler, you go through a lot of flies. You lose them in all the typical ways.

Snagged in a bush.

Snagged on a log in the river.

Snagged in the side of that guy's neck after he tried foolishly to move into the pool you were fishing.

At about a buck and a half each, losing flies can get expensive. Eventually, most fly anglers tire of shelling out their hard-earned cash. The exception would be attorneys, who simply pad the billable hours sheet and buy more flies—which they display proudly on a patch of wool they keep on their dorsal fin and go on catching fish the usual way: in their three rows of razor-sharp teeth.

And so now we venture into one of the oldest, most traditional and enjoyable aspects of fly fishing, a much more enjoyable way to fill our fly box. That's right—during a streamside lunch we take a handful of flies out of our friend's fly box while he's off in the bushes taking a leak.

No, actually, we begin the art of fly tying.

And instead of *buying* flies, we create our own flies—right after we buy two-hundred-dollar stainless-steel vises, delicate feathers plucked from the groin area of Peruvian mountain sparrows, fur yanked from a cheetah's rump by a swift South African tribesman, hooks handmade in Sweden by a man named Sven, who can, in a good week, make two of them, and fly-tying desks made of a certain type of birch that only grows on one hill in a very-hard-to-get-to part of Newfoundland.

By doing that, we will, if we live to the age of 214 and tie flies six days a week, have saved approximately forty-five cents.

Here's just one of hundreds of desks you can purchase to begin tying flies, a desk handmade by the terrific Chilton Co. in Freeport, Maine, and advertised this way: A FLY-TYER'S DREAM.

Imagine my surprise when the advertisement went on and on and nowhere did it mention getting a back rub by the Dixie Chicks.

Anyway, the ad says: "Keep things organized and neat with this handsome birch desk and cabinet. Eight large drawers are lined on the bottom with red cedar to naturally protect your wool, fur, and feathers from moths."

Nothing displeases me, personally, as much as having hundreds in my wool. Never is this more true than when the wool is my long-underwear bottoms, and I am wearing them when the cloud of moths descends from the sky.

This fine fly-tying desk is available, we are told, for $799, plus shipping and handling.

In other words, after you've tied your 350th blue-winged olive, which should take you no more than ten or fifteen years if you have other interests such as *a job*, the damn thing has paid for itself!

Another option is the wonderful fly-tyer's desk made by the equally terrific George D. Roberts Co. of St. Louis, a desk available "in three sizes in oak, cherry, walnut, or the wood of your choice." (My favorite is the wood from the rare ply tree.)

This ad says your family will be proud to have this desk prominently displayed in the home and asks: "Why tie alone in a cold, damp basement or back room?"

Why, you might be wondering, would anyone tie flies alone in a cold, damp basement?

I'll tell you why.

Because your wife just found out you spent this kind of money on a friggin' fly-tying desk while her 1986 Dodge Dart keeps sending up a billowing cloud of orange smoke every time she steps on the gas pedal, her best shoes are held together with a tube of Good, and a month ago you told her that new spatulas are too expensive and she can just turn the kids' pancakes with that broken yardstick that's in the closet.

In an effort to make this section on fly tying more realistic, I will now clamp my own high-tech fly-tying vise to my computer disk and actually try to create some of the flies listed in a fly-tying book.

My vise, by the way, is an expensive English-made model hand-crafted and designed to hold even the tiniest hooks in a firm yet delicate way so as not to stress the fine metal of these hooks.

Oh sure, it may look like a clothespin glued to a sheet of wood from the ply tree, but it is *not*.

Okay, the first fly we will tie is called, I am not kidding, the "PMD Cripple." This fly imitates the pale morning dun and, as a bonus, gets those really good parking spaces right in front of the grocery store.

(Yipes! Was that insensitive or *what?*)

First, according to the book, we will tie the tail and body from pheasant tail. I will do this as soon as I get Max, my Labrador retriever, to stop shaking it.

Okay, now we'll make the thorax of the insect out of yellow Haretron dubbing. Haretron, as you might guess, is made from a rabbit, or hare.

(Dubbing is what they do to make Britney Spears's voice sound a little less like a cat getting its tail stuck under a rocking chair.)

The wing of the PMD is where things really get interesting. According to the book, the only material suitable for the wing is "coastal deer hair."

I am not kidding.

And I'm not sure how one gathers coastal deer hair. Although I'm guessing you might just wait on the beach and hope one washes up after being hit by a ship.

So I have made the tail and body from pheasant tail, lightly coated with dog spit, and tied to a No. 14 Tiemco TMC 100 hook, which is made in Japan by a wuss who apparently couldn't hack the twenty-one-hour days in the Toyota factory anymore.

Then I wrapped the yellow Haretron dubbing and finished it off with the coastal deer hair and voilà . . . I have created what appears to be good-sized moth.

Perhaps that one was a bit too difficult. I'll try a "Hi-Vi Parachute."

Let's see here. This one—I swear I'm not kidding—will require a ft Tiemco TMC 101 hook, gray 8 / 0 thread, and . . . "hackle fibers on a grizzly bear."

(And I thought wrestling that pheasant out of my dog's mouth and yanking a feather out of the bird's ass was a big deal.)

I am reading this fly book, and frankly, I can't seem to find a single fly that can be tied without some degree of danger. The Iso Compara-Nymph, for example, calls for "mallard flank fibers dyed amber." I don't know what kind of company you hang out with, but frankly, I don't want to risk the good-natured ribbing I'd get if any of my friends caught me out in the swamp, rubbing amber dye or, to be honest, rubbing *anything* between a mallard's thighs.

Here's the Royal Double Wing, which requires brown elk hair (make sure not to use the *blue* elk hair that is commonly found on older elk, especially the ones living in Miami) and the following material for the wing: "belly hair from a white-tailed deer."

As I understand it, the accepted way to get this wing material is to dig a shallow hole, about six feet long, in a well-marked game trail. Lie down in the hole, facing up. Keep your hands ready. Then, at some time during the fall or early winter, when a white-tailed deer walks over you, reach up quickly toward the belly, grab a handful, and hang on.

(Important Footnote: If it's a big buck and you grab this handful after most of the deer's underbelly has passed by, especially during the rutting season, you'll *really* need to hang on.)

Finally, here's another fly, one that I have actually tied. It's called the Love Bug, a small bead-head emerger created by a noted fly angler and fly-tyer who goes by the actual name of Trapper Badovinac. (Legend has it he got his name during college, when he actually chewed off his leg to get away from a blind date.)

Anyway, the Love Bug is tied on a tiny, No. 18-22 Tiemco hook and calls for a wing made of partridge feather. (I nearly killed myself when I fell out of the pear tree.)

And the thorax is made from beaver.

As I said, I've tied this fly. I actually used it once, on a stream near my Colorado home. I caught two nice rainbows in the first half hour. Then a knot broke and the fly was free from the tippet. Later that day, however, it came out of the river, gnawed down forty aspen trees, and built a huge dam.

I'm not kidding.

"Your guide will be a little late. His mom is having trouble getting his waders on him."

"$300 for a day's float. $50 more if you want it video-taped, in which case choreography and custom editing will run you a little extra. And of course there's make up, script-writing, costuming . . ."

"You're wasting your time using anything bigger than size 20."

"Quick! Work him around to this side so my logo will show."

"After you revive that six pounder he caught you can revive HIM."

39

White Lies

FOR YOUR BROTHER-IN-LAW

That lure worked before.
Biggest fish ever was caught in that hole.
Fishing is better off the bow.
Come on in, it's not that deep.
I'll pay you back later.

FOR THE WARDEN

It's in my other wallet, pants, in the car, the truck, at home, the
motel, my dog ate it, my wife washed it, and the kids took the
money, too.
I don't know how that got there, never seen that before, nope,
must be someone else's.
This is how we do it back home. We're just saving the smaller
fish so we don't catch them over and over again. We'll let 'em
go later.

FOR YOUR WIFE

That is not lipstick.

CONVERSATION STOPPERS IN THE TAVERN

Non-residents pay your salary.
Husband here, sweet cheeks?
Do you call that a full shot?
Yeah, says who?

Top Ten Reasons Why Fly Fishing Is Better than Sex

Reason #10 | Just getting to the water is highly arousing.

Reason #9 | Fish do not require foreplay.

Reason #8 | A river's sweet spot is easier to find.

Reason #7 | You can do it all by yourself.

Reason #6 | You don't have to take a trout to dinner first.

Reason #5 | You can do it dozens of times a day without tiring.

Reason #4 | You don't have wait for the other person to catch up.

Reason #3 | You can do it in chest waders.

Reason #2 | You don't have to cuddle after release.

And the #1 reason why fly fishing is better than sex . . .
If you break your rod, the company you bought it from will replace it for free.

Troutalope

Habitat: *Wide-open spaces across inland American West.*

Life History: Contrary to common opinion, the troutalope is not rare. In fact, thousands of people have a stuffed one in the garage, bagged with other incredible junk headed to the Salvation Army.

Oh, sorry about that; we were thinking of the jackalope, not the troutalope. Jackalopes are elusive but not rare; not so the troutalope. More in a minute.

The very common jackalope is a mythical animal of North American folklore whose origins date back the Depression years of the 1930s when an underemployed taxidermist in Wyoming (Douglas Herrick, 1920–2003) decided to mount antelope and small deer horns on stuffed jackrabbit heads and sell them to East Coast tourists, like the New Yorker passing through Wyoming in 1935, who spied a *Lepus temperamentalus* in a souvenir shop:

Tourist: Wow! These things really exist!?

Curio dealer: Watching them mate is the most fun.

Tourist [a little embarrassed]: When that happens, which is on top?

Dealer: Well, it ain't the rabbit.

The jackalope's life history is well known: Born the offspring of pygmy antelope and a "killer" rabbit, jackalopes are extremely shy, can be milked (they sleep on their backs and enjoy the fondling), and can be caught with a bottle of Irish whisky.

President Ronald Reagan was given a mounted jackalope by Senator James Abdnor in 1986, but it is not known whether this was just a ceremonial gesture or if the two had been granted hunting licenses and collected the animal legally out in the sagebrush flats far west of the capital to court the gun-rights vote.

We do know that all politicians are hunters when voting season opens and the NRA reaches for its checkbook. In 1993, Bill Clinton bought a hunting license, dressed up in camo, donned waders, and borrowed a Winchester shotgun to go duck hunting. He spent two hours—count them—waiting for a mallard duck to show up. Among the party, a single duck was shot, but the president said he never inhaled—oh, sorry, never pulled the trigger.

Troutalope? Are we making this up?

Of course we are not making this fish up. Truth be known, they still swim freely in many western streams and a few rivers. But they are never caught. Hooked, yes; landed, no.

And here's why.

First, only people with subnormal intelligence are allowed to fish for them legally. And, with an IQ at or below seventy-five, these people are simply too smart to take up fly fishing in the first place.

Second, troutalope are such strong fighters that, should a fly fisherman actually hook one, the odds are 1,000 to 1 against the fish ever being landed. Maybe higher. More than a few anglers have been pulled into deep pools and drowned by these fish—then later found with a broken rod in hand and a grin frozen on their lips.

Why are these fish so strong?

We don't know, but we do know that intelligent fly fishers who target them (illegally) often spend weeks in the Bahamas practicing on tarpon before attempting to take a troutalope.

As one veteran put it, "If you tie a hundred-pound tarpon tail-to-tail with a three-pound troutalope and drop them in the water at the same time, the tarpon will be pulled backward so fast all his scales fly off."

Of some several hundred troutalope hookups, maybe two are ever netted. The rest straighten hooks or break off. And even when brought to the knee for netting, you guessed it, they use their horns to tear a hole in the net to escape.

In one reported case, a fly fisherman claims to have been jabbed in the thigh by a twelve-inch horned troutalope while kneeling to land it—which jabbed holes in his waders, punctured his skin, and sent him to a nearby tavern for medical care where, amid a crowd of skeptics, he attempted to explain how something that looked like a cross between a trout and an antelope had broken his rod and drawn blood.

Sadly, our hero was not successful in convincing his audience about what had happened, but at least he didn't have to pay for his own beer. Following the guffaws and eye rolls, the bartender cried, "The troutalope strikes again, lads! The drinks are on me!"

Some troutalope experts say that new rules may be needed to actually catch these fish.

One example comes from the Alaska commercial fishing fleet, where halibut in excess of eighty pounds are slain by shotgun lest their flopping around on deck break someone's legs.

Naturally, the question has now arisen in fish and game departments all over the West. "Should fly fishers be permitted to use large-caliber firearms to dispatch troutalope before attempting to land them?"

Opinions vary, but fly-shop owners are united against any such nonsense. As one owner put it, "Selling flies is a living; selling rods is a nice living. Brook trout don't break rods, and troutalope do. Killing them would pose a serious threat to our industry."

One final story: It is rumored—only rumored—that Ernest Hemingway hooked several troutalope in his home waters around Sun Valley, Idaho, toward the end of his life.

But he never landed one.

Already depressed, his writing career in shambles, we can only imagine how the great man must have felt after being humiliated by a little trout. In his power years, he had taken great marlin off the stern of the Pilar out in the Gulf Steam west of Bimini while hunting Nazi submarines, and yet here was a bait-sized snippet of a trout mangling his fly rods.

An alleged conversation with the literary giant after a day on the Henry's Fork of the Snake:

"So, Papa, how was fishing?"

"Pretty good. Four browns, two cutthroats, a rainbow . . . and one son-of-a-bitch that broke my rod."

"What could be strong enough to break your rod?"

Hemingway: "Hard to tell. Just slammed my fly and took off. Jumped twice and snapped the bamboo. It was a very good fish and I wanted badly to land it. It was all a fish should be and more."

Then, with the sad eyes of a beaten man, Papa reached for glass of whisky and said, "The goddamn thing had horns."

Coho Salmon Experiment

Mock Fish and Game Announcement

US DEPT. OF FISH AND GAME

The "coho," not being a native of the Lake Michigan water, has experienced difficulty in surviving. The female, when going up the Lake Michigan feeder streams, has been losing her roe on the rocky stream bottom, and, when she got far enough up stream to the small pools and inlets, had great difficulty getting back bunt the mainstream over the sand bars to return to Lake Michigan. In fact, as high as 90 percent were dying at the upper reaches of the Lake Michigan tributaries, which caused an odor problem.

The Michigan sportsmen decided to crossbreed the "coho" with the native "walleye" for two reasons: The walleye (1) knew Lake Michigan tributaries and (2) was not so prone to lose the roe while going up stream. Hence, the name "cowal." This experiment backfired because the fighting coho mixed with the rather sluggish walleye had lost most of the fight the coho was noted for.

In a further experiment, they bred cowal with the greatest freshwater in North America, the "muskie," in an effort to make this double crossbreed the top American game fish. They named this hybrid the "cowalski," and now they have to teach the dumb son-of-a-bitch to swim.

Compiler's note: This bulletin is prime 1970s humor. Apologies to the Cowalski family from Cheese Curd, Wisconsin. No harm was intended. The stadium-sized cheese brat served in the employee cafeteria will be renamed in your honor.

• *43* •

Jetsam and Flotsam

"Anglers are living proof that fish is not good brain food."
—Anonymous

A drunken fisherman checks into his motel room and calls the front desk, saying: "I've got a leak in my sink." Front desk clerk replies: "Go ahead!"

Teacher: Jimmy, if I give you four goldfish today and eight more tomorrow, how many goldfish will you have?

Jimmy: Fourteen.

Teacher: How do you figure?

Jimmy: I already have two goldfish.

A fisherman was trying to teach his son that lying was a sin and that he shouldn't lie about anything, including fishing.

> Father: Do you know what happens to fishermen who lie when they die?
>
> Son: I guess they lie still.

"The only time a fisherman tells the truth is when he calls another one a liar."

The difference between a fairy tale and a fishing story is a fairy tale begins with "Once upon a time," whereas a fishing story begins with "This ain't no b—s—"!

> "My dad used to fish but quit because his net income was not enough." —Anonymous

When big Ole poured out of the tavern and slid down the river back where he often fished, he noticed an old-time baptism service being held on the river. He wobbled over to check it out.

The minister noticed the new prospect and said, "Sir, are you here to find Jesus?"

Big Ole looked at the preacher and said, "Yes, Reverend, I sure am."

The minister then dunks Big Ole under the water, pulls him up, and asks, "Have you found Jesus?"

Big Ole replies, "No."

So, the preacher dunks him again, this time a little longer, pulls him back up, and asks again, "Did you find Jesus?"

Big Ole replies, "No."

By now, the minister is really irritated and he pushes Big Ole's head under water noticeably longer, then pulls him back up and growls, "Now, sir, have you found Jesus yet?"

To which Big Ole replies, wiping his face, spitting water, "No. Are you sure this is where he fell in?"

Contributors

Fishing jokes have a mixed and often unknown parentage. Every effort has been made to track origins. One joke was even tracked to the April 1960 issue of *True* magazine.

Funny fishing stories typically see first light in a magazine, newspaper, and/or book. These contributors were much easier to find, and, if still standing, were generous with permissions. Widows were equally supportive. Ditto for funny fishing cartoonists.

The goal of this book is to highlight and honor select outdoor humorists in print. They are an endangered species, and their ranks are thinning much too quickly. Support their difficult art by buying their books—or at least go to your cupboard to get their poor dog a bone.

"Ex-Angler Is Surviving in a Vegetative State" by Henry Miller. *Statesman Journal,* May 30, 1991. Copyright © by Henry Miller, USA Today Network.

"Channel Fishing" by George Reiger, originally published in *Saltwater Sportsman,* August 2003. Reprinted by permission of the author.

"Mental Health Deflates in Winnebago Sturgeon Shack" © by Dick Ellis. All rights reserved. Reprinted by permission of the author.

"The Marshmallow Purists," "Crazy Fishing," and "Where Are You, Ralph?" from *The Secret Lives of Fishermen: More Outdoor Essays by Jim Dean,* copyright © 2000 by the University of North Carolina Press. Used by permission of the publisher. www.uncpress.org

Acknowledgments

This book would not have been possible without Cynthia Frank, Publisher, Cypress House. Her professional advice, patience, and sense of humor were critical. www.cypresshouse.com

About the Compiler

Brian R. Peterson collects good outdoor humor as a public service. He cannot tell a joke without screwing it up. Spearing Northerns in a dark ice-fishing house is his idea of a Caribbean vacation. He hangs with people who laugh out loud with food in their mouths, and when he recites his last "Now I lay me down to sleep," his hope is a bed of West Coast oysters.